Property of

D0284251

Here at Thy Table, Lord

Property of GREGORY E. POTTS

# Here at Thy Table, Lord

## Alton H. McEachern

Enriching the Observance of the Lord's Supper

**BROADMAN PRESS**
Nashville, Tennessee

© Copyright 1977 • Broadman Press
All rights reserved.

4223-10
ISBN: 0-8054-2310-9

Dewey Decimal Classification: 265.3
Subject heading: LORD'S SUPPER
Library of Congress Catalog Card Number: 77-1024
Printed in the United States of America

To

HOWARD BANKS and OPAL OXFORD McEACHERN
in whose home I learned that
Christ is Lord of the dinner table
as well as Lord of the communion table.

# Preface

I was baptized at the age of twelve and grew up in a fairly traditional Southern Baptist church in Greater Atlanta. Our congregation observed the Lord's Supper quarterly on a Sunday morning. The ordinance was always added onto a full hour service, with the sermon seldom related on the Supper. When I became a pastor seven years later, I followed this same pattern. However, I began to feel that the Supper should be more central in our worship. The sermon should present some aspect of its meaning to prevent the observance from being only an appendage.

In 1966, I became pastor of the St. Matthews Baptist Church in Louisville, Kentucky. They observed the ordinance on the first Sunday of each month. I felt overwhelmed! How could I have a dozen sermons a year on the Lord's Supper, and hope to keep them fresh and meaningful? About that time, J. Winston Pearce's book *Planning Your Preaching* was published, and it had some rich suggestions for preaching on the Supper.

At St. Matthews we moved the observance to Sunday evening on every third month. This allowed for some innovation. My own appreciation for the deep meaning of the communion service grew; and these observances became significant for our members until we could count on an increased attendance when they were announced.

This book is intended to give the pastor ideas for making the observance more meaningful. The first section gives a brief introduction to the theology of the Lord's Supper. The second section suggests ways of varying and enriching these services. The main section of the book consists of devotionals for use at the Lord's table.

I am indebted to Dr. John Lewis, pastor of the First Baptist Church of Raleigh, for the original poem printed as frontispiece. Mrs. Dorothy Holleman has been my helpful typist. The original idea for the book came in conversation with Dr. James Sorrell of Richmond, Virginia, and took its present form at the encouragement of Broadman Press. If pastors find its suggestions helpful and worship is enhanced, my purpose in writing will have been achieved.

ALTON H. McEACHERN

## Abbreviations and Translations

Unless otherwise indicated, Scripture quotations are from the Revised Standard Version, © Division of Christian Education of the National Council of Churches of Christ in the United States of America, 1946, 1952.

| | |
|---|---|
| Barclay | *The New Testament.* © William Barclay, 1968. |
| Jerusalem Bible | *The Jerusalem Bible.* Copyright © 1966 by Darton, Longman and Todd, Ltd., and Doubleday and Company, Inc. |
| KJV | King James Version |
| NEB | *The New English Bible,* © The Delegates of the Oxford University Press and the Syndics of the Cambridge University Press, 1961, 1970. |
| Phillips | *The New Testament in Modern English.* © J. B. Phillips, 1958. |
| TEV | *Today's English Version.* © American Bible Society, 1971. |

## One Loaf, One Body

*One Loaf, One Body offered free,*
*And One Spirit binding all;*
*Because our Savior's parched lips,*
*Drank for us the bitter gall.*

*One Mercy now washing clean*
*Our souls of sin's darkest stain;*
*Because our Savior's riven side*
*Gives to us new life again.*

*One joyful Faith embracing him*
*Who came from heaven above;*
*Because our Savior's dying breath,*
*Grants to us a Father's love.*

*One Hope divine indwelling all,*
*Kept alive by sacred bread;*
*Because our ever-living Christ*
*Rises, Victor, from the dead.*

*One Life, forever fresh and new,*
*Stirs within the wine-red cup;*
*Because our Savior bids us all,*
*With him as Host, now to sup.*

—JOHN M. LEWIS

# Contents

# I
# The Lord's Supper
# in Perspective

It is estimated that some fifty million Americans go to church on a given Sunday. While their motives may be mixed, surely most of them go to worship God. Any activity which involves that many "person hours" is worthy of our best effort. When you consider that it is our central activity designed to honor God, its importance is enhanced even more. Those of us who have responsibility for planning and conducting public worship have an awesome assignment.

Our word *worship* comes from an old Anglo-Saxon word, *worthship*. It means to ascribe supreme worth or importance to God. The psalmist sang, "Give unto the Lord the glory due unto his name" (Ps. 29:2). The author of Revelation sounded the same note when he wrote, "Worthy is the Lamb . . . to receive . . . honour, and glory, and blessing" (Rev. 5:12). The elements of our worship include the reading of the Scriptures, singing hymns and other music, prayer, the sermon, the offering, and times of silence. The observance of the ordinances of baptism and the Lord's Supper are special worship opportunities.

The classic and comprehensive definition of worship is this one from William Temple:

Worship is the submission of all our nature to God.
It is the quickening of the conscience by his holiness;
    the nourishment of the mind with his truth;
    the purifying of the imagination by his beauty;
    the opening of the heart to his love;
    the surrender of the will to his purpose—
And all of this is gathered up in adoration, the most selfless emotion, the chief remedy of that self-centeredness which is original sin.[1]

Spend a devotional period meditating on that definition and you will strengthen your appreciation of worship.

Worship has a dual function. It confronts us with the claims of the gospel and the ethics of Jesus. No person can take the Christ seriously and remain unchanged. (Read the last chapter of Elton Trueblood's autobiography, *While It Is Day*, for an illustration of this truth.) Preach a sermon series on the Ten Commandments and another on Jesus' Sermon on the Mount, and their stark ethical demand will call us to attention.

The second function of worship is to bring comfort to our hurts. "Comfort ye, comfort ye my people, saith your God" (Isa. 40:1, KJV). T. R. Glover is reported to have said he would not give tuppence (two cents) for the man who told him where his duty lies, but he would give all to the man who told him whence his help comes. Worship does both. It confronts the comfortable, and comforts those who hurt.

In our worship we should learn something. Good preaching and worship is didactic; it teaches us. Jesus said to Simon Peter, "Feed my sheep." Worship also causes us to feel something. It calls forth our wonder, excitement, and celebration. Effective worship has a healthy appeal to the emotions; we are stirred and moved. Worship also results in Christian service. It gives us something to do. It calls for action and a change in attitudes. If worship merely stimulates us mentally, it can become coldly intellectual and sterile. When worship is little more than emotional, it degenerates into cheap entertainment or worse. Once knowledge and feeling are coupled with action, life changes occur. The late J. Wallace Hamilton wrote: "Clarity, poetry, vitality—make it clear, make it sing, but above all, make it live!" [2]

The historic word for worship is *liturgy*, which literally means the work of the people. Worship is not a spectator sport with the preacher and musicians as performers. Worship is the work of the people in which they offer themselves to God. The Danish theologian Kierkegaard saw worship as a drama in which the congregation are the actors, the preacher and worship leaders are prompters, and the audience is God. Worship is our offering to God (Rom. 12:1-2). Thus, the assembled church at worship is both a congregation (a human gathering) and a convocation (divinely called together).

Celebration is the essence of our worship. We come rejoicing in God our caring Creator, in Christ our Redeemer who won the victory over sin and death, and in God the Holy Spirit our guide and power source. Of all God's creatures, only men and women celebrate. In both the Old and New Testaments joy and celebration are primary motifs: "You must rejoice at your feast" (Deut. 16:14, *Jerusalem Bible*). "Rejoice in the Lord alway: and again I say, Rejoice" (Phil. 4:4, KJV).

No form of Christian worship is potentially more significant than the observance of the Lord's Supper. It should be the focal point and climax of the service in which it is observed. Since the earliest days of the church's history it has been central in her worship. Henton Davies contends that if preaching is like a radio broadcast of the gospel, then the Lord's Supper is like televising the gospel.

## The Lord's Supper in the New Testament Church

The observance of the Lord's Supper was a central act of worship in the New Testament church. What the Passover meal was to the old covenant, the Lord's Supper is to the new covenant. The church viewed the Supper as a time of thanksgiving. This glad note was sounded when Jesus instituted the ordinance. Paul wrote, "And when he had given thanks, he broke it [the bread], and said, 'This is my body which is for you. Do this in remembrance of me'" (1 Cor. 11:24). Luke gave us a similar report, "And he took bread, and when he had given thanks he broke it and gave it to them, saying, 'This is my body'" (Luke 22:19. See parallels in Matt. 26:27 and Mark 14:23.). In John's Gospel we see this note of thanksgiving in the account of the feeding of the five thousand. Jesus gave thanks over the loaves before breaking and distributing them to the multitude (John 6:11, 23).

The Gospel writers do not tell us the words of thanksgiving or blessing which Jesus pronounced over the bread and cup. One such Jewish blessing common in Jesus' day was:

Praised be thou, O Lord our God, king of the universe,
who brings forth bread from the earth.

Praised be thou, O Lord our God, king of the universe,
   who creates the fruit of the vine.[3]

The early church took up this motif of thanksgiving in their
observance of the ordinance. "And day by day, attending the temple
together and breaking bread in their homes, they partook of food
with glad and generous hearts, praising God and having favor with
all the people. And the Lord added to their number day by day
those who were being saved" (Acts 2:46-47).

Another key word in the New Testament church's understanding
of the Lord's Supper is *koinonia* which means fellowship or participation in the body and blood of Jesus. After his death and resurrection,
Jesus appeared to his disciples at their common meal. In the light
of this fact it is interesting to note that the early church simply
called the Lord's Supper "the breaking of bread" (Luke 24:30; Acts
2:42; 20:7; 27:35). In the observance, believers had fellowship with
one another and with the risen Christ.

Jesus instituted the Lord's Supper at the conclusion of the Passover
meal which he ate with his disciples. (See Joachim Jeremias, *The
Eucharistic Words of Jesus,* pp. 41-63, for a full discussion of the
Last Supper being a Passover meal.) Thus, the Jewish meal of remembrance became the immediate background of the Christian remembrance meal. The Passover commemorated God's deliverance of Israel
in the Exodus (Ex. 12:14). The Supper commemorates divine deliverance of the believer from the tyranny of sin through the death
of the Lamb of God on the cross. The death of the Suffering Servant
was prophesied by Isaiah, "He poured out his soul to death, . . . yet
he bore the sin of many" (53:12). The Passover ends with a shout
and a prayer of praise to God. The Lord's Supper is concluded with
the singing of a hymn of praise. The Passover meal was a commemo-
ration of the old covenant with Israel. The Supper celebrates the
new covenant with the new Israel (the church). As he instituted
the Lord's Supper, Jesus twice mentioned the kingdom of God (Luke
22:16,18). Under the new covenant, kingdom persons experience
genuine worship not in ritual but in a living faith and love. Alan
Richardson contends that the Lord's Supper "is a kind of dramatiza-
tion of the prayer 'Thy Kingdom come.' " [4]

The elements of the Supper are symbols of our Lord's body and blood. A sign or symbol is *semeion* in Greek. A symbol is something which stands for or represents a truth beyond itself. As an example, John's Gospel records seven miracles of Jesus. These were signs of the kingdom and each was an illustration of a spiritual truth. The feeding of the five thousand is a symbol of Jesus saying, "I am the Bread of life." The bread and fruit of the vine are symbols of Christ's body and blood.

These symbols are powerful reminders of our Lord's sacrifice and the high cost of our redemption. They are not "mere symbols" or "bare symbols" devoid of significance. Neither do they possess some magical efficacy. Note 1 Corinthians 10:1-5 where Paul warned the early church that the Supper confers no infallible security to believers. The elements are effective signs when received in faith. Paul regards them as symbols of the "spiritual food and drink" of the new life in Christ (1 Cor. 10:3). Baptism is the symbol of our entry into Christ's body, and the Supper is the symbol of our continuing fellowship with Christ and other baptized believers.

### The Supper's Significance Corrupted

The early church gave a simple and symbolic interpretation to the ordinances. With the passage of time elaborate interpretations were given to the Supper. It was viewed as "the medicine of immortality" and taking the elements was considered essential to salvation. The Supper took on a magical meaning and the grace of God was thought to operate mechanically in the sacrament. The Supper was viewed as a mass in which Jesus was actually sacrificed anew in each ritual. They believed that the elements changed their substance from bread and wine and became the actual body and blood of Christ. Adoration and veneration of the elements themselves bordered on idolatry. Eventually the laity was denied the cup, and was given only the bread. The simple New Testament observance became elaborate and overlaid with superstition. The mass was exalted at the expense of preaching and mystery replaced instruction. The observance became less a grateful remembrance of Christ and more an awesome magical experience.

The Reformation leaders reacted to these corruptions and called for a return to the New Testament understanding of the Supper. The influential layman Zwingli stressed the ordinance as a remembrance of Christ's sacrifice made once and for all, never needing to be repeated. He insisted that the elements were symbols. Baptists' understanding of the Supper's significance is similar to Zwingli's. He was the most effective Reformer in refuting the crude literalism of the contemporary view. He popularized the symbolic interpretation. Along with Zwingli we interpret the words of institution to read "This signifies my body . . . This represents my blood."

D. M. Baillie writes about the Reformed doctrine of the Supper and reminds us that "we stand between a memory and a hope, looking backward to the incarnation and forward to the final consummation.[5] The Supper is a memorial in which we are there—we relive the events on the night of Jesus' betrayal, we stand before the empty tomb on Easter morning, and we are in the upper room at his appearance. We also eat the meal in anticipation of his return at the last trump. C. H. Dodd wrote, "In the Lord's supper we are present at the death of Christ and at His return, at His first and second advent."[6] It is dramatic symbolism, indeed, an "acted parable," a "visible Word." The Supper is a memory, a presence, and a hope.

### A Baptist View of the Lord's Supper

Baptists have taken the doctrinal positions of the Reformation to their logical conclusion. For example, we go beyond an episcopal form of church government, back to the New Testament pattern of congregational polity in which all members have a vote. In its ideal form, our church government is more democratic than any other government on earth. A baptized twelve-year-old member has a vote. The congregation governs itself under the lordship of Christ. Further, Baptists rejected baptism of infants by sprinkling and affusion. We went back to the New Testament pattern of immersion of believers only. Our position is more consistent with the practice of the apostolic church than that of most denominations which grew out of the Reformation.

① Transubstantiation
② Consub — —

In a similar fashion, Baptist understanding of the meaning of the Lord's Supper is more radical than that of other Reformation churches. The Roman Catholic Church holds a doctrine called "transubstantiation." This view contends that the consecrated bread and wine become the literal body and blood of Christ. Martin Luther moderated this doctrine to "consubstantiation." He held that the substances of bread and wine were not changed into (transformed substance) the body and blood. Rather, the body and blood are present with the bread and wine. While John Calvin went further than Luther in modifying this doctrine, he still held that the real presence of Christ was experienced when the believer takes the elements of communion in faith.

Baptists followed Zwingli's lead and went all the way back to what they considered the simple New Testament view: In the observance of the Lord's Supper its elements are symbols of Christ's body and blood. The elements are simply common food. They do not change their substance in any magical or mechanical fashion. They stand for our Lord's body and blood. They remind us of his sacrifice for our salvation. We do not believe Jesus ever intended his words of institution to be taken with crude literalism.

In modern times some Baptists have perhaps gone too far in their insistence that the elements are "mere symbols." This position has caused some people to attach little significance to worship at the Lord's table. It is perhaps natural that our radical rejection of church traditions in favor of the New Testament pattern of faith and practice would lead us to go a bit far in our symbolic view. However, we need to recover the full understanding of the importance of these symbols. A symbol is something simple which stands for something greater (as a flag symbolizes a nation, and a wedding ring symbolizes a marriage relationship). Therefore, we dare not make little of the symbols which stand for our Savior's body and blood.

We believe that we can encounter the risen Christ in our worship. Certainly, we experience his focused presence as we gather about the Lord's table. The Lord's Supper is a symbol of great significance. It focuses our attention not on the elements of the Supper but on the Lord of the table.

This brief introduction to the theology of the Lord's Supper will be amplified in the third section of the book, with its collection of table meditations.

# Notes

1. William Temple, *Readings in St. John's Gospel* (London: The Macmillan Company, 1959).

2. J. Wallace Hamilton, *Still the Trumpet Sounds* (Old Tappan, N.J.: Fleming H. Revell Company, 1970), p. 159.

3. Duke K. McCall, ed., *What Is the Church?* (Nashville: Broadman Press, 1958), p. 81. o.p.

4. Alan Richardson, *An Introduction to the Theology of the New Testament* (New York: Harper & Bros., 1958), p. 368.

5. D. M. Baillie, *The Theology of the Sacraments* (New York: Charles Scribner's Sons, 1957), p. 102.

6. C. H. Dodd, *The Apostolic Preaching and Its Development*, p. 235.

# II
# Meaningful Ways
# to Vary the Observance

*In recent years, Baptists seem to be giving greater emphasis to significant and beautiful observances of baptism and the Lord's Supper. Although reacting against a sacramental view of the ordinances, we see them as having a symbolic interpretation in the New Testament. When Jesus said of the Lord's Supper elements, "This is my body" and "This is my blood" he was speaking symbolically.*

## Preparation for Observing the Lord's Supper

The frequency of observing the Lord's Supper varies widely, usually monthly or quarterly. Perhaps bimonthly would be a good way to have the Supper, plus special observances. In recent years some churches have begun observing the Supper on Maundy Thursday. (Thursday before Easter was the day Christ instituted the observance with his disciples in the upper room.)

It can be helpful to have the service at various times. It can be held at morning worship and become the focal point of the service. This may be varied by having it on Sunday evening or at the midweek service, occasionally. Some churches observe the ordinance on Christmas Eve or on the Sunday before Christmas. Thanksgiving eve is also an appropriate time for a special service.

The service can be varied by changing its location. In addition to using the church sanctuary an evening service can be held in the chapel or fellowship hall. Some churches have the Supper around the table following a church dinner or love feast. Try having the service out-of-doors, on the church lawn, or in a secluded location in a park or forest. The early church must have met like that for many years before they owned a building of any kind.

In many churches the pulpit may be removed and the communion table put in its place for the observance. Simple but attractive art can add to the service. A poster board may depict a loaf or a grape cluster. A single loaf of bread may be used in the observance to emphasize our unity in Christ. A long table can be placed at the front of the church, with eleven deacons seated at it to represent the apostles.

Some churches broadcast their observance on a local radio station or on television. On that Sunday the deacons go by twos and observe the Supper with shut-ins while listening to the broadcast. This is meaningful both to the shut-in members and to the deacons who serve.

Deacons should be carefully organized and trained for participation in the observance of the Lord's Supper. Their purpose should be to serve the congregation smoothly and with reverent simplicity. Everything should be carefully prepared well ahead of time to avoid any embarrassment.

### A Regular Lord's Supper Service

Once the devotional or sermon is concluded, a period of silent prayer and quiet music may follow. Then let the pastor and deacon chairman or staff minister remove the covering cloth from the table. (Some churches omit the use of that cloth.) The pastor asks a blessing on the bread. Then it is given to the deacons and they serve the congregation. When the deacons return to the front with the remaining elements, they are given to the pastor and chairman and are placed on the table. Then the pastor serves the deacons, and the deacon chairman serves the pastor.

The pastor takes the bread and repeats Jesus' words, "This is my body which is for you." The congregation eats the bread simultaneously.

In a similar way the cup is served to the congregation following a prayer of blessing. The people retain their cups while the pastor quotes Jesus, "This cup is the new covenant in my blood. Do this as often as you drink it, in remembrance of me." The congregation drinks the cup simultaneously.

The cups are either placed in holders on the back of the pews or collected by the deacons. The table is re-covered with the cloth by the pastor and chairman.

Customarily a hymn follows. It may be a hymn of invitation or dedication. As the congregation leaves the sanctuary some deacons stand at the doors to receive a fellowship or benevolence offering. This offering dates from the time of the early church and is used to aid those who are in need. Many churches administer the benevolence offering confidentially through a deacon committee.

### Making the Observance Meaningful

The Lord's Supper can be served following a baptismal service. It is beautiful to observe the two New Testament church ordinances in the same worship service. Let them be the worship service. Baptism may open the service and the observance of the Lord's Supper conclude it.

Newly baptized members may sit on the front pew to receive the Lord's Supper for the first time. The pastor should serve them, and they may keep their communion glass as a reminder of their initial observance. If small silver cups are used, they may then be engraved with the name or initials of the candidate and the date of their baptism. These prove to be treasured keepsakes.

Another way of adding to the significance of the Supper is for the pastor to read an invitation to the Lord's table just prior to serving the elements.

### The Setting

The observance should be held with reverence and served with dignity. Every effort should be made to set the mood for this most significant worship opportunity. This can be aided by having dim lighting or candlelight, soft music, and quiet speaking. Care should be given to select appropriate music for the observance. It can reinforce the thrust of the message. Make use of hymns of consecration. A choir and soloists may sing appropriately during the serving. At some time the service, perhaps on Sunday evening, might use all spontaneous music.

The pastor should select and read appropriate Scripture passages as part of the observance. Some of these include Luke 22:7-22, John 6:58, Hebrews 9:22, 1 John 1:7, 1 Corinthians 11:23-26, 28-29, Matthew 26:26-28, Mark 14:22-24, Luke 22:17-19, and 1 Corinthians 10:16-17. The pastor should practice reading the passages to stress their meaning. No form of proclamation is more appropriate or powerful than the Scriptures well read or recited.

## Worship Centers

Worship centers can add to the beauty of our observance. Obviously, there are many ways in which they may be prepared.

For instance, on a table behind and above the communion table place a large open Bible, elevated toward the congregation. Put a scarlet, purple, or gold cloth underneath the Bible. It could be made of satin or velvet. Put a large red ribbon in the Bible as a marker.

Some churches have a bronze cross with candlesticks on either side, as a worship center.

At the Easter season place a large cross behind the table or in the baptistry opening. Place Easter lilies at its base, as a symbol of the resurrection. The cross might be spotlighted from the balcony.

Flowers can make a beautiful interest center. At the Christmas season use poinsettias and at the Easter season use white lilies.

One pastor places the Lord's Supper elements beside the table and uses it as a worship interest center. Using boxes and satin cloth, he builds two levels on the table. On the top level he places a large silver goblet, and on the lower level a silver tray with a loaf of home-baked bread.

## A SERVICE AT THE LORD'S TABLE

**PRAISE BE TO GOD**
　PRELUDE　　　　　　　　　　　　　　　　　　Organist-Pianist
　CALL TO WORSHIP (adapted from Isa. 55:6-7; Pss. 24:3-4; 51:10-12)

*Minister:* Seek the Lord while he may be found; call upon him while he is near.

*People:* Who shall ascend the hill of the Lord? And who shall stand in his holy place?

*Minister:* The person who has clean hands and a pure heart, who does not lift up his soul to what is false, and does not make dishonest promises.

*People:* Create in us clean hearts, O God, and renew a right spirit within us. Restore to us the joy of our salvation, and uphold us with a willing spirit.

*Minister:* Let the wicked forsake his way, and the unrighteous man his thoughts, and let him return unto the Lord, and He will have mercy upon him, let him come again to our God, for He will abundantly pardon.

　INVOCATION—Lord's Prayer—"Doxology"
　HYMN

**IN REMEMBRANCE OF CHRIST** (observed by candlelight)
　JESUS' INVITATION TO COMMUNION　　　　　　　　　Minister
　HYMN
　PASTORAL INVITATION TO THE LORD'S TABLE
　ORDINANCE OF THE LORD'S SUPPER

**MINISTRY OF THE WORD**
　SCRIPTURE LESSON　　　　　　　　　　　　　　　　Minister
　CHORAL MUSIC　　　　　　　　　　　　　　　　Adult Choir
　　　"When I Survey the Wondrous Cross"
　SERMON　　　　　　　　　　　　　　　　　　　　Minister

**WORSHIP IN COMMITMENT:**

*Minister:*   Behold, the Lamb of God, who takes away the sin of the world!

*People:*   Have mercy upon us and grant us peace.

*Minister:*   Loving Father, take our hands which have held holy things and labor through them.

*People:*   Take our lips which have tasted the symbols of the body and blood of our Lord and speak through them;

*Minister:*   Take our bodies which have received these symbols of bread and wine and make them temples of your spirit;

*People:*   Take our minds and think through them;

*Minister:*   Take our hearts and fill them with your love that we may truly serve you in this community and the world. Amen.

HYMN            "I Surrender All"

**AFFIRMATIONS AND BLESSINGS**

SCRIPTURE                      Isaiah 55:10-12                      Minister

*Minister:*   The peace of our Lord Jesus Christ be with you all.

*People:*   Peace be with you.

*Minister:*   Worthy is the Lamb who was slain;

*People:*   The Son of God who gives power and wisdom and blessing.

*Minister:*   Beloved, Christ has risen.

*People:*   The Lord has risen indeed. Hallelujah!

*Minister:*   Christ has been raised from the dead, first fruits of those who have fallen asleep.

*People:*   Thanks be to God, who gives us the victory, through our Lord Jesus Christ.

BENEDICTION                                                        Minister


—Ken Altom, *Eden, North Carolina*

## SUNDAY EVENING OBSERVANCE
## OF THE LORD'S SUPPER

SACRED ORGAN MUSIC
A CALL TO WORSHIP from Isaiah 55
HYMN OF GOD'S LOVE                                St. Catherine
    "Jesus, Thy Boundless Love to Me"
INVOCATION and LORD'S PRAYER
HYMN OF GOD'S LOVE                                St. Margaret
    "O Love That Wilt Not Let Me Go"
READING OF THE WORD No. 84
SOLO   "Alas! and Did My Saviour Bleed?"          arr. Reynolds
A CALL TO PRAYER

> *Minister:* Our Father, we come knowing that we have failed in so many ways this week.
>
> *People:* Sometimes we have tried to hide from you, from one another, and from ourselves.
>
> *Minister:* There have been times when we have drawn back from the right because it was a difficult, demanding experience.
>
> *People:* Too often we have involved ourselves in meaningless rounds of activities that lead nowhere.
>
> *Minister:* We have strayed far from the fullness of life that you have made possible for us.
>
> *People:* Give us now the grace to accept the healing of our brokenness and the prospect for new birth.
>
> *Minister:* Let us now privately confess our own sins.

SILENT CONFESSION OF SIN
EVENING PRAYER
HYMN OF GOD'S GRACE                               Moody
    "Grace Greater Than Our Sin"

THE EVENING OFFERING
    Cello Offertory
    Offertory Prayer
MEDITATION                  "You Are There"              Minister
HYMN OF INVITATION                                       Aurelia
      "I Lay My Sins on Jesus"
THE SHARING OF DECISIONS
OBSERVANCE OF THE LORD'S SUPPER
    *Receiving the Bread*
      Music:              "None Other Lamb"          Marshall
                  Sanctuary Choir
    *Receiving the Cup*
      Music:              Organ Meditation
A PARTING HYMN              "I Will Sing of My Redeemer"

## SUNDAY AT THE WHITE COLUMNS

SACRED ORGAN MUSIC      "Fugue in G Minor"      Charpentier
† WORDS OF WELCOME
  Guests are invited to meet the pastor and Mrs. McEachern in
  the church parlor following morning worship.
† CONCERNS OF THE CHURCH
CHORAL CALL TO WORSHIP
      "The Lord Is in His Holy Temple"              Root
INVOCATION
†° HYMN FOR THE NEW YEAR                      Cwm Rhondda
    "Guide Me, O Thou Great Jehovah"
ORDINANCE OF BAPTISM                      Dr. McEachern
SCRIPTURE READING                      Matthew 21:28-32
CALL TO PRAYER
MORNING PRAYER
†° HYMN OF COMMITMENT                          Arlington
    "Am I a Soldier of the Cross?"

Radio Greeting

THE MORNING OFFERING

*Offertory Music*          "Sarabande"          J. S. Bach

 \*Gloria Patri*

 \*Prayer of Dedication*

SERMON          "Profession and Practice"          Dr. McEachern

ORDINANCE OF THE LORD'S SUPPER

 *Giving of the Bread*

 *Giving of the Cup*

"I Saw the Cross of Jesus"          Mayfield

Sanctuary Choir

\* HYMN OF INVITATION          Wellesley

"There's a Wideness in God's Mercy"

FELLOWSHIP OFFERING

SHARING OF DECISIONS          BENEDICTION

CHORAL AMEN          ORGAN DISMISSAL

\* The congregation will stand.  †Ushers will seat people at this time.

## ORDER OF SERVICE

A TIME OF REVERENCE AND PERSONAL PRAYER
*The Prelude*
*Hymn:*      "Into the Woods My Master Went"    S. Lanier

A TIME OF SELF-EXAMINATION
Do I realize that I am a sinner?
Do I know that I cannot merit God's love, and
yet he loves me still?
Do I know that my hope is in his grace?
Do I love myself more than Christ, more than others?
Do I live up to the vows I made when I became a
member of the body of Christ?
*Hymn:*

A TIME OF FORGIVENESS
O God forgive me for . . . . . . . . . . . .
Help me to see my real needs, and the needs of others.
I acknowledge that I do not have all the answers,
but you are the answer.
Forgive me for using instead of loving others.
Forgive me for living as though you were dead;
at times I am a practical atheist.
Forgive me when I follow the ways of my culture instead
of your ways.
Forgive my pride, my greed, my hatred and selfishness.
O God, may I forgive others, as you have forgiven me.
Prepare me to sit at your table.
Through Jesus Christ our Lord. Amen.
*Hymn:*

INVITATION TO THE TABLE

Jesus said, "Come unto me all ye that labor and are heavy laden and I will give you rest . . ."

"Behold, I stand at the door and knock . . ." God has showed his love for us "in that while we were yet sinners, Christ died for us."

"This do in remembrance of me."

Let us come and receive his grace, his forgiveness, his love and strength. As we remember that Christ died for us, so let us be aware that we are in his Presence.

*Anthem:*

SCRIPTURE

"Now as they were eating, Jesus took bread, and blessed, and broke it, and gave it to the disciples and said, 'Take, eat; this is my body.' And he took a cup, and when he had given thanks he gave it to them, saying, 'Drink of it, all of you; for this is my blood of the covenant, which is poured out for many for the forgiveness of sins. I tell you I shall not drink again of this fruit of the vine until that day when I drink it new with you in my Father's kingdom' " (Matt. 26:26-29).

SHARING THE BREAD

"This is my body. This do in remembrance of me."

SHARING THE CUP

"This cup is the new covenant in my blood which is shed for many for the remission of sins. This do in remembrance of me."

A TIME OF DEDICATION

*Hymn*        "Blest be the Tie"        Dennis

*Benediction*    Congregation prays the Lord's Prayer

*Choral Amen*

The Service Begins When the Worship Ends.

## A SILENT OBSERVANCE

There will be no speaking during our worship experience. Read,
sing, and pray in silence. Let us pray that our deepest needs
will be met as we do this in remembrance of him.

MUSIC FOR MEDITATION
  *Ladies Handbell Choir*        "Prelude on St. Anne"        Young
MEDITATION FOR LORD'S SUPPER                                Chilcotf
  "At twilight hour the burdened Savior came with his disciples
to the upper room. The feast was spread, soft-lit by oil lamp's
flame. Each sensed the presence of impending doom. 'This is
my body; take, and eat,' he said; 'And drink the cup; my blood
for you outpoured.' And as they ate and drank, their hearts he
read and found not one to him securely moored: one would betray,
another would deny, And one escape from dark Gethsemane;
And one, unsure of self, said, Is it I? The unpossessed of Christ
thus never see! Possess us, Lord, for otherwise we're lost; Infuse
Thyself with us at Pentecost!"

PRAYER OF INVOCATION                    Offered by each in silence
  We seek the blessedness of your presence, our Father, as we
approach that mystic experience of communion with you. Consider
our meditation. Touch us with a feeling of your realness so that
we may know that we are your children. In the name of Christ
our Lord. Amen.

HYMN OF COMFORT           "Abide with Me"           Sung silently
ORGAN INTERLUDE
THE WRITTEN WORD                    Based on Mark 14:12,17,22-24
                                               1 Cor. 11:25-28
  On the first day of the Feast of Unleavened Bread . . . When
it was evening, Jesus came with the twelve disciples. While they
were eating, Jesus took bread, gave a prayer of thanks, broke it,

and gave it to his disciples. "Take it," he said, "This is my body."

Then he took the cup, gave thanks to God, and handed it to them; and they all drank from it. Jesus said: "This is my blood which is poured out for many, my blood which seals God's covenant.

"Whenever you eat the bread and drink the cup, do it in memory of me." For until the Lord comes, you proclaim his death whenever you eat this bread and drink from this cup . . . Everyone should examine himself, therefore, and with this attitude eat the bread and drink from the cup.

THE EVENING OFFERING

*Ladies Handbell Choir*      "The Lord's Supper"      Van Hemert
*Offertory Prayer*

We thank you for the many blessings that are ours through Jesus Christ, our Lord. Amen.

HYMN OF THE LORD'S SUPPER                          Sung silently

PRAYER OF CONFESSION AND BLESSING               Offered silently

Father God, give me grace so that I may draw near to Thy table in faith, not trusting in my own righteousness, but in Thy mercy. I acknowledge my sins before Thee. I pray for the strength to amend my ways. As I eat of this bread and drink of this cup, bring to my remembrance Thy love by which I am redeemed through Jesus Christ, my Lord. Amen.

RECEIVING OF THE BREAD

"Take, eat: this is my body, which is broken for you."

RECEIVING OF THE CUP

"This cup is the new testament in my blood shed for many for the remission of sins . . . drink ye all of it."

HYMN OF BENEDICTION                               Sung silently

SILENCE AND THE SANCTUARY CHIMES

In the name of the Father, the Son, and the Holy Spirit

". . . THEY WENT OUT."                    Let us depart in silence.

## CHRISTMAS EVE COMMUNION

A lovely and meaningful time in which to observe the Lord's Supper is on Christmas Eve. Such a service could be held at various hours, even midnight. Consider a 5:00 P.M. service. That hour has several advantages: persons can attend en route home from work and it is ahead of family observances and dinner. In the winter it is not dark as the service begins, but is dark by its close and the time for candle lighting.

A suggested order of service follows:

SACRED ORGAN MUSIC
CHORAL CALL TO WORSHIP
      "Let All Mortal Flesh Keep Silence"      Holst

> Let all mortal flesh keep silence,
> And with fear and trembling stand;
> Ponder nothing earthly-minded,
> For with blessing in His hand,
>
> Christ our God to earth descendeth,
> Our full homage to demand.

INVOCATION
CAROL      "Hark! The Herald Angels Sing"      Mendelssohn
LADIES HANDBELL CHOIR
      "Angels We Have Heard on High"      arr. Stephens
CAROL      "O Little Town of Bethlehem"      St. Louis

"THEY ENCOUNTERED HIM"

| | | |
|---|---|---|
| JOSEPH | *Monologue* | Ken Brannon |
| MARY | "My Joy, My Love" | Susan Long |
| | with choir | arr. Salsbury |
| PETER | *Monologue* | Phil Anderson |

"We Encounter Him"

FLUTE ENSEMBLE AND ORGAN
　　　　　　"Come unto Him"　　　　　　　　　Handel
OBSERVANCE OF THE LORD'S SUPPER
　*Giving of the Bread*
　　　　　"I Wonder as I Wander"　　　　Appalachian Carol
　*Giving of the Cup*
　　　　　"Sweet Little Jesus Boy"　　　　　MacGimsey
ANTHEM　　　　"Praise Ye the Lord of Hosts"　　Saint-Saens
　　　　　　　　Service Choir
LIGHTING OF THE CANDLES
　　　　"Joy to the World! The Lord Is Come"　　　Antioch
BENEDICTION


*Notes on the Observance:*

Consider having the congregation fill the pews from the front. This may be accomplished by roping off the back or side areas. The candle-lighting is most impressive when the worshipers sit close together.

The handbell choir or antiphonal choir may be placed in the balcony or at the back of the congregation. This can add to the impressiveness of worship.

The monologues may be presented by persons in costume. They may use the ones on the following pages or they can write their own with imagination. Their presentations should be limited to three to five minutes each.

In place of the flute ensemble, you could substitute cello, violins, or other appropriate instrumental music.

During the observance, the pastor and deacon chairman (or a staff minister) serve in the accustomed manner. The pastor may choose to give a brief devotional before the Supper, or let the monologues be the spoken devotional thought. If he does the latter, he should have some transitional sentences about "We Encounter Him" at the table. Note the special music coincides with the distribution of the bread and cup.

If there are newly baptized converts present, have them sit on the front pew. Let the pastor call their names as he serves them the bread and cup (after he has served the deacons). He may want to say something like, "James Phillips, I am pleased to serve you the Lord's Supper for the first time, following your baptism. Take this bread (cup) in remembrance of him."

After the observance and anthem, distribute trays of small candles (with cardboard shields to protect the hands from hot wax) to the deacons. Let each person in the service take a candle. As the deacons return to the front, collect their trays and give each one a ten-inch white candle. After the pastor or worship leader lights his own candle, he then lights the candle of the deacon chairman. Simultaneously, they light the deacons' candles. Then the deacons pass up the aisles, lighting the candles of worshipers who sit at the end of each pew. Each person's candle is lighted from that of the person sitting next to him, and he passes the light along until all hold a burning candle.

When every worshiper's candle is burning and the deacons have returned to their places, stand and sing, "Joy to the World! The Lord Is Come."

As a benediction, ask the worshipers to lift their candles above their heads. Then the worship leader will say: "And Jesus said, 'Ye are the light of the world! Let your light so shine before men that they will see your good works, and glorify your Father, who is in heaven.'"

Obviously, many variations may be made on this order of worship. Certain adaptation will be required to make the observance significant in a given congregation.

### Joseph's Monologue

"When Mary told me of how the Lord had chosen her for this great thing that was to be, I was dismayed, and I must admit, filled with disbelief. I'm ashamed to say it now, but I felt angry, disgraced, and betrayed. All the plans I had for the two of us to begin our lives together seemed to have no meaning. How could she really expect me to believe such a thing?

"I had decided to have our marriage contract put aside quietly, when an angel came to me in a dream to reassure me. Indeed, it was exactly as Mary had told me. O God, forgive my disbelief. I should have known that Mary would not lie!

"Mary was so content, even happy. I had such misgivings about being the earthly father of this heavenly child. O God, how could I guide him? What could I teach him? How could a simple carpenter provide for his needs? I'm just making a name for myself as a carpenter. I had hoped to have a son who would work beside me in my shop, but surely God wanted more for his Son than this.

"Rome had ordered everyone to go to the city of his birth to be counted and taxed. It would have been a difficult journey for us anytime, but with Mary's time so near it was almost impossible. We had a donkey for her to ride and although it was cold and the road was rough, Mary never complained. The roads were filled with people headed for Bethlehem, and we passed inn after inn where there was no room. Mary's time grew nearer, and I would have begged if it had been necessary to find for her a warm, dry place to have the child.

"The innkeeper was so busy that he hardly saw us. He gave us what he had. It was only a stable, but it was warm and dry and the sweet-smelling hay piled on the hard earthen floor made a fine bed for Mary. The animals were quiet and still as I fixed the manger for the child.

"When the baby was born, Mary wrapped him in swaddling clothes and laid him in a manger. When I saw him, I was filled with indescribable joy. Anyone who has seen his firstborn knows this joy, but this was Jesus. He was so small. I took his tiny, soft hand in my rough calloused hand—and suddenly my fears vanished and a quiet confidence and rejoicing filled my heart. As the tiny finger grasped my hand, I knew—this is Jesus.

"I spoke his name and how I loved him."

Kenneth Brannon
*Greensboro, North Carolina*

*Peter's Monologue*

"I, Peter, 'the rock,' I denied him—Jesus—not once, but three times. Just as he predicted. Why? Why? I loved him—oh, how I loved him. I suppose it was fear that made a coward and a liar of me.

" '*I never knew him!*' Yet ever as I spoke those words and warmed myself by *their* fire, he looked at me with love and understanding. That look . . . his look . . . it . . . broke . . . my . . . heart. If I had not been such a coward, I might have done as Judas; instead, I wept bitterly.

"I left him to die—alone. I was sure that this was the end of all of us. But the Lord, you see, had plans for me.

"I remember that day—that dear and precious day. The sun was high, and the gulls filled the air with their cries and the flapping of their wings. The sky was azure blue, and the sea a deep blue-green. There we sat, my father, my brother, Andrew, and myself.

"Mending the nets was a tedious job, and as Jesus approached us no one looked at him directly. Yet when he spoke with that calm, compassionate voice, both my brother and I stopped our work.

"Jesus presented an interesting challenge: 'Follow me, and I will make you fishers of men.'

"I looked at Andrew, and he looked at me, and we both looked into the water. Then we just had to laugh because it sounded so absurd.

"Yet strange as it may seem, I got up and left my nets. I followed Jesus to the synagogue, where he spoke. His words stirred me deeply and I knew that this was no ordinary man.

"In the days that followed, he proved to us what I already knew. Certainly no ordinary man could calm a troubled sea and cause an emotional weakling like me to walk upon the water! What man could heal the sick and blind, and even bring people back from the dead? And who do you know that radiates love for all mankind, especially the weak, outcast, and downtrodden?

"Though I marvel at all of this, I marvel more at what he did for me. Jesus took me just as I was—a cocky, impetuous, self-confident, rough fisherman—and he shaped me and molded me with his love, and patience, understanding. He taught me stability, humility, and the real meaning of service. He gave to me the joy of the presence of his Spirit, and the privilege of sharing his love and salvation.

"He not only let me be a fisher of men, but also feed his sheep, and invite others to come unto him!"

Phil Anderson
*Greensboro, North Carolina*

## A Maundy Thursday Variant

On the Thursday evening before Easter, have the congregation gather for the observance in a church fellowship hall. Arrange tables in the shape of a cross. On the table at the center of the cross place an open Bible, and perhaps three burning candles to symbolize the Trinity. (A candle is a symbol of the burning presence of God, the Shekinah glory.)

Give each worshiper a plate with a small loaf of bread, and a small glass of grape juice. Instead of dark Concord grape juice, use the red. Let the music focus on the cross and sacrifice of Christ. Familiar hymns may be used to avoid use of a hymnal. Special music should be appropriately chosen.

The pastor then reads selected Scripture passages which relate to the cross. He gives an eight- to ten-minute devotional based on the crucifixion. Then the words of institution are given: "This is my body . . . this is my blood . . . . Do this in remembrance of me." The congregation eats the bread and drinks the juice until all of it is consumed. Soft music may be played.

After a prayer of benediction, the people go out in silence. They may give their offering as they leave the service. Have receptacles placed at the entrances, such as an offering plate on a low stand, with a piece of purple velvet beneath the plate.

In larger congregations it may be necessary to have two or three services. Divide the congregation alphabetically. Those with last names beginning with A through N come at one hour. Those with M through Z at the next hour. While the service may only last for thirty to forty minutes, allow time between the services to refurbish the table.

Make effective use of lighting. Let the room be dimly lit to add to the atmosphere of reverence. A spotlight could be used to highlight an interest center such as the open Bible or a large mounted cross. Women of the church might bake the small loaves or a commercial bakery could supply them.

### Maundy Thursday Prayer

Let us recall the words Jesus spoke from the cross:

"Father, forgive them: for they know not what they do."

We thank you, Father, that Jesus did as he told others to do, and forgave those who wronged him. Help us to forgive others from our heart. And forgive our world for still committing acts of great cruelty.

"Truly, I say to you, today you will be with me in Paradise."

We thank you, Father, that Jesus gave this assurance to a man convinced he deserved to die. Awaken us and all sinners to a true understanding of what we are and what we have done. But give us, too, the same assurance, that whatever we have done nothing can separate us from your love.

"Woman, behold your son. Behold your mother."

We thank you, Father, that Jesus thought of others even when dying. Deliver us from self-pity, from brooding on our own wrongs and misfortunes. Help us to be like Christ to our neighbor, acting as Jesus would act, mediating your love.

"My God, my God, why have you forsaken me?"

We thank you, Father, that Jesus was fully human, and no stranger to the anguish of despair. Help us through the dark times, so that we may emerge with faith strengthened.

"I thirst."

We thank you, Father, that someone answered this cry. Help us to answer the cry of those in our world who are hungry and thirsty and in need.

"It is finished!"

We thank you, Father, that Jesus died believing he had done your will and accomplished your work. May we, too, be single-minded, and when we die not need to regret that we have squandered your gift of life.

"Father, into your hands I commit my spirit."

We thank you, Father, that Jesus died trusting fully in you. May all Christians have the same confidence in the hour of death. May we know that Jesus has conquered death for us all.

Through Jesus Christ, our Lord. Amen.[1]

## WHEN THE DEVOTIONAL FOLLOWS THE OBSERVANCE

(The first part of the service consists of congregational singing, special music and the offering.)

PRAYER "Almighty God, unto whom all hearts are open, all desires known, and from whom no secrets are hidden, cleanse the thoughts of our hearts by the inspiration of the Holy Spirit, that we may perfectly love thee and worthily magnify Thy holy name; through Jesus Christ our Lord. Amen."

APPROACHING THE TABLE

In a premarital conference the bride said to her pastor, "We want our wedding to be very simple and very sacred." That is a good description of the Lord's Supper. It is a very simple observance, using the common elements. Yet, it is as sacred as the body and blood of our Lord. Let us draw near in faith.

As we approach the table let us hear the Word of God.

From the Old Testament: Exodus 20:2,7-17.

From the New Testament: 1 Corinthians 11:23-26,28.

THE BREAD

Jesus took the bread, blessed it and broke it and passed it among his disciples.

Father, bless this broken bread to remind us of the body of our Lord, given for us. (The bread is served to the congregation.)

"This is my body which is for you. Do this in remembrance of me." (The bread is eaten in unison.)

THE CUP

Jesus took the cup, blessed and passed it among his disciples.

Father, bless this cup as a sign of our unity, and our Lord's life, given for us. (The cups are served to the congregation.)

"This cup is the new covenant in my blood. Do this . . . in remembrance of me." (We drink the cup in unison.)

(After the observance, the devotional follows.)

Once a man arrived late at church. People were leaving. He asked an usher, "Is the service over?" The usher replied, "Worship is over, the service has just begun." Worship and work, liturgy and life are parts of a whole. If we only pray and worship, we become too heavenly minded and neglect the practical application of the gospel. If we simply go into the world and serve, neglecting prayer and worship, we become shallow and humanistic. We must balance life and liturgy (or worship). Elton Trueblood contends this balance is as essential as breathing in and breathing out.

We came to the Lord's table in self-examination and repentance. Now we go out to serve the Lord by helping others. Here eternity intersects time. In our worship we have heard a Voice from beyond saying,

"This is my body . . . . This is my blood.

This is for you . . . . Do this in remembrance of me."

At the table we've encountered the Man from Galilee, the Christ of Emmaus, the Prince of peace. Here we have been reminded that we are not our own, and we go out to live as those for whom Christ died.

That night, after the Supper was instituted, Jesus said to his disciples, "Arise, let us go." They sang a hymn and went out to the garden of Gethsemane—and beyond.

We leave the Lord's table and go out to apply the gospel ethics to life, and to share our faith. We have gathered to pray, now we go out to serve the Lord by serving our fellowman.

Now the service begins!
HYMN OF INVITATION
RECEIVING NEW MEMBERS
BENEDICTION

## READINGS FOR USE AT THE LORD'S TABLE

At the table of the Lord Jesus Christ
> We look back,
>> and see the goodness and mercy which has followed us
>> all the days of our lives.
> We look forward,
>> in anticipation that great far-off divine event toward
>> which all creation moves.
> We look about us,
>> and have fellowship with our fellow born-again believers.
> We look inward,
>> examine ourselves, confess our sins, and receive the
>> assurance of divine pardon.
> We look out,
>> and long to see our kith and kin, friends and family
>> come to know and love the Lord.
> Let us worship God
>> here at the Lord's table.

This reading may be given by the minister or a layman prior to the observance. It may also be printed as a responsive reading with the congregation saying, "We look back, we look forward, . . ." and the worship leader or choir reading the following response.

### Readings at the Table
> *Leader:*  In a time of sorrow, a time of despair;
> *People:*  We have come to celebrate the Word.
> *Leader:*  In a time of confusion with our world in turmoil and

our lives torn between issues:

*People:*    We gather as a congregation to celebrate the Word.

*Leader:*    In a time when our various worlds are hungering and thirsting for love, forgiveness, grace, and goodness;

*People:*    We have come to rededicate our lives to the task of putting our flesh in the Word.

*Leader:*    In the midst of flashing neon darkness,

*People:*    We dare this day to celebrate the light.

*Leader:*    In the midst of blaring, shouting silence,

*People:*    We dare this day to celebrate the word.

*Leader:*    In the midst of bloated, gorged starvation,

*People:*    We dare this day to celebrate the bread.

*Leader:*    In the midst of bottled, bubbling thirst,

*People:*    We dare this day to celebrate the water.

*Leader:*    In the midst of smothered, gnawing doubt,

*People:*    We dare this day to celebrate the affirmation.

*Leader:*    In the midst of frantic, laughing death,

*People:*    We dare this day to celebrate the life.

*Leader:*    Sing alleluia—rejoice! Christ is here!
             Let us join him at his table.[2]

### A Doctrinal Summary

A variant preparation for observing the Lord's Supper is to have the congregation read a doctrinal summary in unison. This could consist of key Scripture verses. One way to do it is to modify the "Apostles Creed" (which was not written by the apostles). An example follows:

### WE BELIEVE

We believe in God the Father Almighty, Maker of heaven and earth; And in Jesus Christ, his only Son, our Lord
Who was conceived of the Holy Spirit,
Born of the virgin Mary,
Suffered under Pontius Pilate, was crucified, dead and buried;
Who was raised from the dead on the third day,

Appeared to many and ascended into heaven,
Who sits at the right hand of the Father.
And who is coming again to judge the living and the dead.
We believe in the Holy Spirit,
The church as the body of Christ,
The forgiveness of sins, the resurrection of the dead, and life eternal.

### Church Covenant

As we come to the table together, let us hear the reading of our Church Covenant and be reminded of our common bonds:

"As we trust we have been brought by divine grace to embrace the Lord Jesus Christ, and by the influence of his spirit to give up ourselves wholly to him, so we do now solemnly covenant with each other that, God helping us, we will walk together in him in brotherly love;

"That, as members one of another for the glory of Christ in the salvation of men, we will exercise a Christian care and watchfulness over each other, and as occasion may require, faithfully warn, rebuke, and admonish one another in the spirit of meekness, considering ourselves lest we also be tempted;

"That we will willingly submit to, and conscientiously enforce, all wholesome discipline of the church;

"That we will uphold the worship of God and the ordinances of his house by regular attendance thereon, search diligently the Scriptures, observe closet or family worship, and seek to train up those under our care to the glory of God in the salvation of their souls;

"That, as we have been planted together in the likeness of his death by baptism, and raised from an emblematic grace in newness of life, especially will we seek divine aid to enable us to walk circumspectly and watchfully in the world, denying all ungodliness and every worldly lust;

"That we will remember the poor, and contribute cheerfully of our means for their relief, and for the maintenance of a faithful gospel ministry among us, and for the spread of the same to the ends of the earth;

"That we will endeavor, by example and effort, to win souls to Christ; and,

"Through life, amidst evil report and good report, seek to live to the praise of him who hath called us out of darkness into his marvelous light to whom be glory and honor and power for ever and ever, Amen."

## INVITATIONS TO THE LORD'S SUPPER

Friends, if you sincerely turn your back on your sins, if you want to live in love and peace with everyone, if you desire to lead a new life doing God's will from now on, then prepare to receive this ordinance. Now let us make our peace with God, confident of his forgiveness, by joining in this prayer of confession:

O God, whom Jesus called Father, we admit that we have done many wrong and wicked things. We admit that we have ignored many opportunities to do the loving thing. We are sorry that we have thought, said, and done such foolishness. Now we turn away from our mistakes. We are sick at heart, Father, when we think of them. Forgive us for not knowing what we do. Please forgive us. In the name of Jesus, forgive us. Grant that we may so love and serve you all our days, that others will come to know, love, and praise you. Amen.

### Words of Assurance

God our Father has promised to forgive all who turn to him in faith. Even now he forgives us and sets us free to live new lives in Jesus Christ our Lord. Henceforth we may live, not in fear or dread, but secure in his power and love. Nothing can separate us from the love of Christ. Therefore, let us rejoice in the Lord our God about his table!

### Jesus' Invitation to Communion

On many occasions, Jesus encouraged people to draw near to him
for communion and strength. Even now he invites us into his
presence with these words:

"If anyone thirst, let him come to me and drink. Whoever drinks
of the water that I shall give him shall never thirst; the water
that I shall give him will become in him a spring of water
welling up to eternal life. He who believes in me, as the scripture
has said, 'Out of his heart shall flow rivers of living water' "
(John 7:37; 4:14; 7:38).

"I am the bread of life; he who comes to me shall not hunger and
he who believes in me shall never thirst (John 6:35). I am the
living bread which came down from heaven; if any one eats
of this bread, he will live forever; and the bread which I shall
give for the life of the world is my flesh. He who eats my
flesh and drinks my blood has eternal life, and I will raise him
up in the last day. For my flesh is food indeed, and my blood
is drink indeed. He who eats my flesh and drinks my blood
abides in me, and I in him (John 6:51, 54-56).

"Come to me, all who labor and are heavy-laden, and I will
give you rest" (Matt. 11:28).

### Pastoral Invitation to the Lord's Table

You who truly and earnestly repent of your sins,
    who stand in a right relationship with your neighbors,
    who pledge to live a new life in Christ,
    who intend to follow the commandment of God
        and live by Christ's ethic:
    Now draw near with faith to his table,
    and take these sacred symbols of his body and blood,
    confess and repent of your sins,
    find comfort and encouragement in your needs,
    Through Jesus Christ, our Lord.

## PRAYERS AT THE LORD'S TABLE

### In the Spring
"Lo, the winter is past
  the rain is over and gone;
  The flowers appear on the earth;
  the time of the singing of birds is come" (Song of Sol. 2:11-12).
Father, we rejoice in the beauty of the good earth
  and in the beauty of worship.
The Lord's table reminds us that we owe you an unpayable debt
  for creation—we owe our existence to you;
  for redemption—the gift of Christ's body and blood;
  for your providential care and guidance.
Here we celebrate your mighty acts on our behalf and
  we await the quiet working of your Spirit,
  calling us to faith and to follow.
As we have fellowship with other baptized believers
  about the table, make us mindful of our larger kinship
  which reaches around the world
  through Jesus Christ our Lord. Amen.

### Christmas Communion
Lord Jesus Christ, Prince of peace, be born in our world anew,
  Where there is hostility and war,
  Where there is pain and heartbreak,
  Where there is no hope.
Come Lord, with healing and with help.
Dear Lord, this Christmas
  Open our eyes to thy glory
  Open our ears to the angel's song
  Open our hearts to thy transforming love.
Come thou Light of the world and shine in the darkness

of our sin and doubt.
Here at thy table, come to us
 with forgiveness for our sins,
 with grace to enable us to cope,
 and with sheer joy. Amen.

### Bible Sunday

 "Holy Bible, Book divine,
  Precious treasure, thou art mine:
  Mine to tell me whence I came:
  Mine to teach me what I am."
Dear Father, we thank you for your Book, our Bible
 For those you inspired to write it,
 For those who translated it into our mother tongue.
 For scholars whose devout and careful study
  open its meaning to us.
Help us to read and study the Scriptures,
 to apply their truths to our daily life, and
 to discover your person and will in the written Word.
Now, as we come to thy table, may we encounter thy Son,
 the living Word. Amen.

### Our Interdependence

Father, we thank you that there are some things we do alone,
 we offer our private prayers,
 we decide our personal faith,
 we sing solos.
We are also grateful there are some things we do with others:
 we join in corporate prayer,
 we worship around the Communion Table,
 we perform an oratorio.
Remind us of our common debt and dependence on others
 and those with whom we share our common faith in Christ
  as Messiah.
 In his name we pray. Amen.

### We Come to the Table

Father, we come to you in *Praise*
    for your creative power,
    for your sustaining grace,
    for your redeeming love.
We come to ask your *Pardon*
    for our insensitivity to our neighbor's need and hurt,
    and for our preoccupation with self and self-interests.
We pray in *Petition*
    for your presence in our worship and
    for your power in our daily lives
    through the Lord Christ. Amen.

### The Unexpected

Father, here at your table we are grateful
    that life is just as filled with unexpected joys as sorrows.
    We know we will always have problems—that's life.
    But we also know we will always have you—and that's life
      abundant.
As we worship you through the observance of the Supper
    May we be surprised by joy;
    the joy of your grace,
    the joy of your presence,
    the joy of your love,
Here we see the reflection of your face and
    we feel your nearness
    as your glory passes by
    through our Lord Jesus Christ. Amen.

### The Saints

Here at thy table, Lord, we are grateful for the church triumphant,
    gathered in heaven's grandstand, watching how we run faith's
      race.
We give you thanks for those who went before,
    for those who converted our ancestors
    and brought the gospel to these shores.

Make us equally faithful in sharing the faith in Jesus' name. Amen.

### The Gate of Heaven

"Surely the Lord is in the place. How awesome is this place!
This is none other than the house of God, and this is the
gate of heaven."
Father, we come into your presence, here at the table.
We confess our failure to love, which is sin. Forgive us.
Grant us wisdom to know the right, and courage to do it.
Enlighten our minds with your truth;
Encourage our hearts with your love;
Endue our lives with your power,
And make our worship acceptable in your sight. Amen.

### Pilgrim People

Father, here at your table eternity intersects time and
we are aware that:
We are pilgrims here; heaven is our home.
We are Christian soldiers, make us loyal to you our King.
We are your disciples, make us apt learners and faithful
witnesses.
Forgive us when we are intolerant, quick to take offense,
and slow to understand;
When we put self-interest above your interest.
Bless those whom we love, kith and kin, friends and family.
Bless all who need your grace today
those who are ill and in pain
sad and lonely
poor and in need.
May we help to answer this prayer by sharing encouragement,
sympathy, and our gifts.
Our hearts are filled with gratitude
for your provision of all our needs
for all life's extras, your Word, your Son, your Supper.
Accept our thanksgiving and praise
through Jesus Christ our Lord. Amen.

*Prayer Preceding the Supper*

The worship leader may read some classic Christian prayers at the observance. A couple of examples follow:

### St. Patrick's Prayer

Christ with me, Christ before me, Christ behind me,
Christ in me, Christ beneath me, Christ above me,
Christ on my right, Christ on my left,
Christ when I lie down, Christ when I sit down,
    Christ when I arise,
Christ in the heart of every man who thinks of me,
Christ in the mouth of every one who speaks of me,
Christ in every eye that sees me,
Christ in every ear that hears me.

### St. Francis' Prayer

Lord,
Make me an instrument of Thy peace;
Where there is hatred, let me sow love;
Where there is injury, pardon;
Where there is doubt, faith;
Where there is despair, hope;
Where there is darkness, light; and
Where there is sadness, peace.
O Divine Master,
Grant that I may not so much
Seek to be consoled as to console;
To be understood, as to understand;
To be loved, as to love;
For it is in giving that we receive;
It is in pardoning that we are pardoned;
It is in dying that we are born to eternal life.

St. Francis' prayer has been set to music. It could be sung by a choir or soloist, just before the observance.

## Notes

1. C. Micklem, *More Contemporary Prayers* (Grand Rapids: Wm. B. Eerdmans Pub. Co., 1970), pp. 77-78.
2. David J. Randolph, *God's Party* (Nashville: Abingdon, 1975), pp. 21-22.

# III
# Meditations
# at the Lord's Table

## 1. Remember Jesus Christ
Luke 24:13-35, Phillips

At sunrise on Sunday morning, December 7, 1941, three-hundred and fifty Japanese war planes flew through a mountain pass on the island of Oahu and rained death and destruction on Pearl Harbor. Eight battleships and ten smaller warships were sunk or put out of commission. Two hundred American planes were destroyed and 3,581 servicemen were killed or wounded. The USS *Arizona* took a bomb down its stack. The boilers, oil tanks, and munitions magazine exploded! The battleship went down in eight minutes, entombing 1,177 sailors. President Franklin D. Roosevelt called the day of the sneak attack, "a day of infamy." The national battle cry with which the United States entered World War II was, "Remember Pearl Harbor!" That was our nation's motto until V.J. Day, September 2, 1945.

Today the rebuilt country of Japan is the world's third industrial power. The Arizona memorial is visited by one million tourists each year, many of them Japanese. Hawaii is a state and its governor, one of its U.S. senators, both its congressmen, and the president of the University of Hawaii are of Japanese descent.

There have been other battle cries in our two hundred-year history such as "Remember the Alamo!" and "Remember the *Maine!*"

The Lord's Supper is not a battle cry, but it, too, is a call to remembrance. "Remember Jesus Christ!" could well become our motto. It means more than merely recalling Christ. It is a call to renew, rekindle, relive the total Christ-event.

54

## I. Remember Who Jesus Is

① He was the son of Mary. His favorite name for himself was "Son of man." Jesus was a man, very human, and one with us. The Lord's Supper and our faith are rooted squarely in the midst of history. Jesus was disappointed when the multitudes went away. He asked if his disciples would leave as well. Peter rose to the occasion when he responded, "Lord, to whom shall we go? You have the words of eternal life" (John 6:68). Jesus was tempted, as we are. The account of Jesus' bout with Satan in the wilderness must have had Jesus himself as its source. He shrank from suffering just as we do—recall his experience in the garden of Gethsemane. Jesus was a man.

While Jesus was fully human, he was more. He was also the divine Son of God. He is the cosmic Christ who came from heaven's glory into this world of suffering. He was co-creator with the Father and Spirit, and he came into the world to redeem it. "To wit, that God was in Christ, reconciling the world to himself" (2 Cor. 5:19).

We dare not deny either Jesus' humanity or his deity. To do so is heresy. Jesus is both. "Remember Jesus Christ."

## II. Remember What Jesus Did

He came to earth. He was born in Bethlehem, grew up and became a working man in Nazareth, was baptized in the Jordan River, carried out his ministry in Galilee and Judea, and was crucified outside Jerusalem.

Jesus came to show us the Father. He showed us that God is caring and approachable, that there is no limit to divine love, no cost it will not bear for our salvation. Once a famous theologian lectured in Edinburgh, Scotland. Afterward an ordinary Scottish woman said to him, "I do not understand all you say when you preach. But I can tell you are making God great!" Jesus was clearly understood by his hearers and he "made God great." A boy once said that Jesus is the best picture God ever had taken.

Jesus came to die, for us. An Appalachian carol, whose author is unknown, expressed this idea beautifully:

> I wonder as I wander out under the sky
> How Jesus the Savior did come for to die
> For poor on'ry people like you and like I,
> I wonder as I wander out under the sky.[1]

At the Lord's table we "Remember Jesus Christ," who came and died for us.

### III. Remember Where Jesus Is

He is at the Father's right hand in glory. He was exalted after the resurrection and he carried humanity into the Godhead. Even so he will come at the end of the age, to judge the living and the dead.

Jesus is on the earth today in the person of the Holy Spirit. The Scriptures equate the Holy Spirit and the Spirit of Jesus. In John 14 he promised to send us "another comforter" (Paraclete). Christ is here in believers. Our bodies are the temple of his Spirit: "Christ in you, the hope of glory" (Col. 1:27, KJV).

Jesus is here, at his table. He is not in the bread and cup in any magical sense. But he meets us in a real and mystical fashion when we observe this remembrance service. Just as surely as he was with his disciples at the table in the upper room, so his focused presence is with us, as his disciples, here at the communion table.

The observance of the Lord's Supper is a confession of our common faith in the Lord Christ. As we take these elements let us "Remember Jesus Christ."

Now as we come together at the table let us repeat quietly and in unison:

"*Remember* Jesus Christ,
Remember *Jesus* Christ,
Remember Jesus *Christ!*"

## 2. Love's Memorial
1 Corinthians 11:23-26

The immediate setting for the first observance of the Lord's Supper was the Jewish Passover. This was an annual feast of remembrance. Its purpose was to commemorate the passing over by the death angel of Jewish families in Egypt, prior to the Exodus. The meal was a celebration of God's deliverance from slavery and the formation of the Jewish nation.

The Passover was a real meal which was celebrated corporately and not privately. There had to be at least ten persons present at the observance. The ingredients of the meal were prescribed and each had a highly symbolic significance. There was unleavened bread. Because the Hebrews had to leave Egypt in haste, there was not time to wait for the bread to be leavened. There was a bowl of salt water to remind the celebrants of the tears their ancestors shed while in slavery, and as a symbol of their miraculous crossing of the Red Sea. On the table were bitter herbs, such as horseradish, to remind them of the bitterness of bondage in Egypt. A paste of apples and nuts was served, along with cinnamon sticks. The paste was symbolic of the clay from which their forebears had made brick, and the cinnamon sticks represented the straw used in making the bricks. Cups of wine reminded the worshipers of the joy of deliverance.

On Thursday of Passion Week, Jesus and his twelve disciples ate the Passover meal together in the upper room in Jerusalem. That night the atmosphere in which they observed the feast was charged. There was impending disaster. Within the group there was strife over the personal ambitions of the disciples. Betrayal was about to take place. Jesus also foretold the disloyalty and denial of Simon

Peter that night.

There were fearful dangers from without. Jesus' enemies were determined to see him dead. The scribes and Pharisees viewed him as a lawbreaker whose popularity threatened established religion. The Sadducees and Herodian party saw him as a rebel who was about to incur the wrath of Rome on the country. The priests felt that Jesus was not sympathetic to the Jewish sacrificial system from which they gained their livelihood. He represented a serious threat to his enemies, and they were determined to eliminate him. Jesus' triumphal entry into Jerusalem and his cleansing of the Temple of its money changers and merchants sealed his doom.

It was at the Passover observance on that poignant Thursday evening that Jesus instituted the Lord's Supper. He used two of the items on the table, bread and wine, to initiate the Christian memorial meal. What does the Lord's Supper mean to us as Christians?

## I. The Supper Is a Revelation

It stabs us awake, calls us out of our complacency, and reminds us of the costliness of our salvation. We forget so easily. The human mind is like a writing slate, easily erased. We become preoccupied. The periodic observance of the Lord's Supper brings us back to center, forces us to focus on the heart of our faith. These elements, loaf and cup, vividly portray Jesus' sacrifice for us. Memory hears the cries of the crowd, the drip of water in Pilate's basin, the crack of the whip, and the thud of the hammer. Memory sees the flickering torches, Judas' dark kiss, and the towering cross with its Suffering Servant. Memory recalls all this.

The Supper forces us to look back and remember what God in Christ has borne that we might be saved. Someone once asked a master musician, "What's the good word for today?" He struck a tuning fork and replied, "That's A! It was yesterday and will be tomorrow. It will still be A a thousand years from now. The soprano may be off key, the tenor flat on the high notes, and the piano out of tune, but that is A." The Lord's Supper is God's A, to remind us of what is most important. It brings our faith into focus.

## II. The Supper Is a Realization

Christ is not a dead hero to whom we build a monument. He is not an embalmed leader. A communist once taunted a Christian saying, "We have Lenin's body on display in his tomb. All you Christians have is an empty tomb!" Precisely! Jesus is not dead but alive! We serve a living Lord who was not only back there, but is here as well. You see, we still meet him and have fellowship with him. The human-divine encounter still occurs. J. B. Phillips calls the Lord's Supper "an appointment with God." He confronts us here at his table, in the midst of our work and our worship. Just as we accept his salvation, so we appropriate his presence, in our observance.

The risen Christ is here. See his revelation. Eat these elements in remembrance of him. Realize his presence.

Come, let us worship in the glad fellowship of the table.

*Prayer:*

Come, Holy Spirit, heav'nly Dove
With all thy quick'ning pow'rs,
Kindle a flame of sacred love
In these cold hearts of ours.

# 3. The Lord's Supper in Three Tenses

"The cup of blessing which we bless, is it not a participation in the blood of Christ? The bread which we break, is it not a participation in the body of Christ? Because there is one loaf, we who are many are one body, for we all partake of the same loaf. So, whether you eat or drink, or whatever you do, do all to the glory of God. For as often as you eat this bread and drink the cup, you proclaim the Lord's death until he comes" (1 Cor. 10:16-17, 31; 11:26).

No service of Christian worship is more sacred, holy, or meaningful than the observance of the Lord's Supper. No doctrine is more misunderstood than this. Some appear to make too much of it. They observe it every day of the week, consider the sacrifice of Jesus to be repeated in every observance, and believe the bread and wine become the actual body and blood of Christ by a miracle. On the other hand, some Christians seem to make too little of the observance. One denomination does not celebrate the Lord's Supper at all. Others consider it a mere symbol, practically devoid of meaning. The biblical understanding of the Supper's significance lies between these extremes.

## I. The Supper Points to Christ's Past Sacrifice

"Do this in remembrance of me."

There was the shadow of a cross across the table that night in the upper room. Jesus was keenly aware of what was at hand for him: "He riseth from supper, and laid aside his garments; and took a towel and girded himself" (John 13:4, KJV). This observance looks back to that infamous hill called Golgotha outside the city wall. Here we commemorate that cosmic conflict between good and evil, God and Satan.

At the Lord's table we call to mind the high cost of our salvation. While it is free to us, it cost Christ dearly—his very body and life's blood. In the Old Testament, worship centered in the sacrifice of unblemished lambs. John the Baptist pointed Jesus out saying, "Behold, the Lamb of God!" Jesus was God's provision for our redemption and Calvary was his high altar.

We look back toward Calvary with wonder and gratitude. We eat this symbolic meal in remembrance of him and his sacrifice. He died to set us free.

## II. The Supper Points to Christ's Presence with Us Now

This observance is not simply keeping a dead memory alive. It is entering into the presence of One who lived, died, was raised from the dead by the power of God, and is alive forevermore. Above that, he is present with us here and now—at the table. While we recall that great past event and victory, we also enjoy the presence of the risen Christ in our worship. We have "communion" (1 Cor. 10:16) with him, as well as with fellow believers.

The church is not an organization whose purpose is to keep alive the memory of a hero out of the ancient past. It is an organism, a living entity in which we have fellowship with our living Lord. Let us never relegate him merely to being back there. He is here, as well. You cannot embalm him in history. His bones are not blowing in the dust of Palestine. He is here and his Word is relevant to our deepest needs and hurts, today. Never forget that we celebrate the Lord's Supper in the present tense.

### III. The Supper Points Us to Christ's Future Return

"For as often as ye eat this bread, and drink this cup, ye do shew the Lord's death till he come" (1 Cor. 11:26, KJV).

You proclaim the Lord's death *till he come.* Did three words ever tell more? There is a forward look, a future stance to our worship today. We observe the Supper here in the midst of history, with an eye to the end of history and our Lord's triumphant return. This is the church's glorious hope.

The Christ who was born at Bethlehem, crucified on Calvary, and raised on the first Easter morning is coming again. The risen Christ with whom we have fellowship here at the table is going to return to earth visibly and in victory. He will come again as Judge and King. This promise is enough to give us bright hope in the darkest hour.

A friend visited in wartorn Poland in 1950. He told about a church building which had been reduced to rubble by repeated bombing. The postwar congregation was too poor to buy new materials to rebuild the church. They broke the rubble into smaller pieces, mixed it with concrete and rebuilt the church. Over the door they wrote the Latin words: *Sursum Corda*—lift up your heart!

The observance of the Lord's Supper is a *sursum corda* experience. It is a time to lift up our hearts to the glad hope and sure promise of Christ's return. "Lift up your heads; for your redemption draweth nigh" (Luke 21:28, KJV). Never forget the triumphant future tense of the Supper. We will one day be forever with him and the redeemed of all the ages.

We remember with gratitude God's provision in the past.

We enjoy Christ's presence with us in the present, and

We rejoice in faith's future promise of Christ's return.

Let us come to the table now that we may be strengthened in our faith, comforted in our sorrows, inspired for life's brave journey.

*Sursum Corda!*

## 4. Acted Parables

Actions speak louder than words. We've all heard that old but accurate adage. An old Chinese proverb reflects this idea:

"I hear and I forget;

I see and I remember;

I do and I understand."

Old Testament leaders and prophets knew this truth. After Joshua led the children of Israel across the river Jordan into the Promised Land, he had them build a heap of twelve large stones. This was to serve as a visual reminder of the providence of God on their behalf. When their children would ask, "What mean these stones?" their fathers could tell what God had done. (See Josh. 4:19-24.)

Isaiah received a message from God and proclaimed it, but the people refused to listen. So the prophet found an innovative way of preaching. He went to a festival or fair and sang a love song. Because everyone loves a lover, the crowd gathered round to listen. Isaiah sang "the Song of the Vineyard" (5:1-2), and in the third verse he said, "You are the vineyard of the Lord" which proved so disappointing. He went on to pronounce the judgment of God on Judah, unless they repented. (Read this parable in the *Good News Bible*.)

Jeremiah was perhaps the most vivid Old Testament prophet. He used a number of dramatic actions to illustrate and drive home his message. He accused his disobedient generation of being like a vine with no grapes. He illustrated their hardness of heart with the story of the potter and his clay pot (see chap. 19). He said they would be like sheep scattered by lions (50:17).

Jesus was the Master Teacher who knew the value of an acted parable. His words were memorable and his parables stick in our minds. Yet, his actions speak louder still.

## I. "He Took a Child" and Taught Trust (Mark 9:33-37)

Jesus illustrated true greatness by taking a child as an example. The point was not the child's innocence. Which of us could approach that? Such would be a depressing lesson. The point Jesus was making was a child's wide-eyed wonder. We are to stand in awe at the mysteries of life, such as birth and love and death. Or consider a child's utter dependence on its parents. We are to rely on our Father's providential care and undeserved love in much the same way. Or again think about a child's implicit trust, which never doubts and seldom worries. We, too, can commit all our life to God's care. May we have the child's simple faith in our heavenly Father. "He took a child." What a simple yet profound example.

## II. "He Took a Towel" and Taught Humility (John 13:3-5)

The disciples did not learn very well, it seems. They were filled with contention and selfish ambition. They were anxious for the chief places in Jesus' kingdom. Just at that point their Master, keenly conscious of his own lordship, took a towel and washed their dusty feet. "He best honors God who stoops and serves." What a blow to their pride that must have been!

The Suffering Servant's insignia is not a crown or scepter, but a towel and basin—or worse, a criminal's cross. On that cross time and eternity intersect and the God-man brings man and God together. What a lowly and yet powerful insignia. What symbolizes your life? Is it your automobile or sports trophies? Is it your beautiful house? What is your insignia? "He took a towel."

### III. "He Took a Cup" and Gave Us a Sermon in Action

Bread is the staff of life, but this bread on the Lord's table represents the Bread of life which satisfies man's higher hunger. Eating bread together symbolizes our friendship, and Jesus called us not slaves but friends. This communion bread is broken to remind us of his body which was broken for us on the tree.

The cup is also a sign of suffering. Recall how he prayed in Gethsemane, "Let this cup pass from me!" The cup is symbolic of Christ's life poured out from the cross.

> But none of the ransomed ever knew
> How deep were the waters crossed;
> Nor how dark was the night that the Lord passed thro'
> 'Ere He found His sheep that was lost.
>
> ELIZABETH C. CLEPHANE

The cup is, further, a symbol of our unity in Christ. The one cup stands for our oneness in him.

"Drink ye all of it," Jesus said.

Who can forget the way in which Jesus taught trust, humility, and love?

"He took a child."

"He took a towel."

"He took a loaf, a cup."

Let us now take these simple elements, bread and a cup, and remember with gratitude our living, returning Lord.

*Prayer:*

> Father, give us
>    a child's wonder,
>       that the loveliness of the world may be to us forever new;
>    a child's forgiveness,
>       that we may forget injustice and unfairness,
>       as a child forgets;
>    a child's obedience,
>       that as a child obeys a father,

we may obey you;
a child's trust,
that as a child trusts his parents for everything,
we may commit our lives in trust to you. Amen.[2]

# 5. This Is the Life

God is Spirit and animals are body. But man is both spirit and body. He is made in the image of God and yet he is a creature. We are not to despise material things, for God made them, too. Christianity has been called the world's most materialistic religion. The practical elements of the Lord's Supper remind us of the historical nature of our faith. It is not some visionary otherworldly affair. God is concerned about the here and now as well as the hereafter. He is equally the maker of earth and heaven. Never forget that God loves this world and men supremely (John 3:16).

## I. The Lord's Supper Is Witness to History

As we take it, we proclaim the historical fact of our Lord's death. The Bible and our faith are anchored squarely in the midst of time. They are not merely mystical or philosophical. Rather, Christianity is concrete and rooted in historical time, places, and persons. God is not only supra (above) history, he is also in it. Christ on the cross was not doing a piece of Docetic playacting. Nor was he some kind of Gnostic phantom who only appeared to suffer and die. He was real, fully human, and the Gospel accounts of his suffering are factual. In 1 John 5:6-8 we have three witnesses who testify to the historicity of the Christ-event: the Holy Spirit, the water of our baptism, and the blood of the Lord's Supper, and "these three agree."

As we take the Lord's Supper we proclaim our Lord's saving death.

In our own strength we are helpless to save ourselves. We cannot be different, better, clean, or pure. Left to his own devices, man thinks he can change the world and himself, but he is sadly mistaken. "Simply do the loving thing," we are told. But such a statement reflects a naive view of human nature. By what stretch of the imagination do we presume that we are capable of knowing and doing the loving thing in each life-situation? Left to human resources alone we would find "Truth forever on the scaffold, Wrong forever on the throne."

But don't despair. There is a land of beginning again. We can be better than we are. It is possible to be forgiven and pure again. This is the good news of the gospel. By faith in Christ we can be made new.

In the Lord's Supper observance we experience vicariously the Christ-event and he is known to us in the breaking of the bread. Therefore:

## II. The Lord's Supper Is a Witness to Hope

While it is an historical celebration, it points beyond history to the eschatological truth of Christ's return. As believers in Christ, we will be participants in those great events of the end time. Our God has a goal for history and mankind and it is the kingdom, the consummation on the Day of the Lord (*Yom Yehweh*). Just as an expectant mother carries her child with such anticipation, so the Christian lives in hope of that day when faith will give way to sight.

Thus, we are reminded that our faith has a forward stance. At the Lord's Supper we are present at Jesus' death and we know we will be present for his return. We are by faith participants in both his first and second advent. When Christ returns, he will deliver us from temptation, evil, and sin. We will also be set free from all pain, suffering, and limitations. We will hear Jesus say, "Come, O blessed of my Father, inherit the kingdom prepared for you from the foundation of the world" (Matt. 25:34).

The Supper points back to Christ's death, and it points forward to his return. It holds the past and the future in the now of faith.

As we prepare to come to the table let us look inward. It may not be a pretty sight. We are selfish, proud, and prejudiced in many ways. We may be guilty of being cold, and narrow in our affections. Often we are insensitive to the hurts and needs of others, uncaring and indifferent. At times we have not been honest with God, others, or ourselves. Now is the time to confess our sins and receive divine forgiveness.

We examine ourselves and approach the table in fellowship with our Lord. Following the Supper we sing a hymn and go out to love and help, to share Christ and serve.

Let us celebrate this historical and the hope-filled Supper.

# 6. Guests of God

The Lord's Supper has been given many names throughout Christian history. These include communion, which means fellowship with or participation in. It has been called the Eucharist, which is from the transliteration of the Greek word *eucharistia* meaning thanksgiving. ("He took the cup and gave thanks.") It is called the sacrament, from the Latin word for a soldier's oath of loyalty, *sacramentum*. Some call it the *agape* or love feast. It is also called simply the breaking of bread or the Christian Passover. All these designations have significance and enlarge our understanding of the Supper.

We come to the table as the guests of God and feel the claim of this ordinance on our conscience and our loyalty.

## I. There Is an Upward Thrust

The Supper has a vertical dimension as we are drawn into fellowship with Christ. After all, it is the Lord's table, not ours or our church's. The first direction of this observance is upward, toward the Lord. He is the host here and we are his guests. Psalm 23 expresses the gracious generosity of God as not only our shepherd but also

our host: "Thou preparest a table before me in the presence of mine
enemies: thou anointest my head with oil; my cup runneth over.
surely goodness and mercy shall follow me all the days of my life:
and I will dwell in the house of the Lord for ever" (Ps. 23:5-6,
KJV). At the table we participate in the fellowship of his body and
his blood (Eph. 2:13).

While it is important that born-again believers gather at the Lord's
table, many denominations try to build fences about the observance.
They seem to delight in restricting it and defining who can partake.
One denomination has each member visited by deacons to evaluate
their spiritual qualifications and actually issue tickets to the table
which are taken up when members take communion.

Never forget, this is the Lord's table, not ours.

## II. There Is an Inward Thrust

The observance of the Lord's Supper is an intensely personal
spiritual experience. That is why the apostle Paul instructed the
early church, "Everyone should examine himself, therefore, and . . .
eat the bread and drink from the cup. For if he does not recognize
the meaning of the Lord's body when he eats the bread and drinks
from the cup, he brings judgment on himself as he eats and drinks"
(1 Cor. 11:28-29, TEV).

Partaking of the Lord's Supper calls for taking a spiritual inventory.
It is a time to let the searchlight of God shine into every dark recess
of our soul. It calls for confession of our sins, renewal of our vows,
and experiencing the forgiveness of God here at the table.

## III. There Is Also an Outward Trust

While the observance calls for the closest personal self-examination
and confession, it does not stop there. The Supper is more than
a time for spiritual navel-gazing. Just as our vision is focused on
Christ and on ourselves, so it is also focused on other persons. We
do not eat this symbolic meal alone. There is no such thing as Lone
Ranger Christianity. We may pray in a closet, but we take communion along with other believers. It is a corporate act. It is an ordinance
of the church, not of individuals. Therefore, it is not something we

do in isolation but in fellowship with other Christians.

We also observe the Supper as an act of Christian witness. It has an evangelistic purpose. "As often as you eat this bread and drink the cup, you proclaim the Lord's death till he comes" (1 Cor. 11:26). In the observance we not only bear witness to God's grace to our fellow believers, but to nonbelievers as well. The Supper is a graphic way of saying, "Look! See how much God cares for you. Look at the lengths to which he went for you to be saved! This is his body which was broken for you, too. This is his blood which was shed for you. Look and believe. Look and be saved."

The upward look shows us our gracious Savior.

The inward look shows us ourselves as sinners whose repentance results in forgiveness.

The outward look shows us our fellow believers and the unsaved for whom he also died.

Look and live. You are the guest of God here at his table.

# 7. Three Suppers

Though it is an everyday experience there is something special about eating together. We do not normally eat with persons whom we do not like, or with whom we do not have a relationship. Many clubs and groups are built around table fellowship. The Lord's table is central in the architecture and worship of the church. Eating is prominent in the Scriptures, and there are three suppers or banquets which stand out. These meals have special significance.

## I. The Old Covenant Meal (Ex. 24)

In about 1250 B.C. the Exodus of the children of Israel occurred. They came out of Egyptian bondage into the desert to the east. At Mount Sinai, God cut a covenant with his chosen people. Taking the initiative, he promised to be their God, provided they were obedient to his law. "Then he [Moses] took the book of the covenant, and read it in the hearing of the people; and they said, 'All that the Lord has spoken we will do, and we will be obedient'" (Ex. 24:7). The covenant was an agreement between God and his people with God as the senior partner. It was conditional depending on their obedience. Their special relationship with him was not due to their goodness, but to his grace.

The covenant at Mount Sinai was sealed by the eating of a meal in the presence of God. "They beheld God, and ate and drank" (Ex. 24:11). In a sense the annual Passover feast continued to be the meal which celebrated and recalled the Exodus from Egypt and the covenant relationship of the chosen people with God.

We know from studying the Old Testament that Israel was not faithful to the covenant nor were they obedient to the law of God. Therefore, they were taken into captivity in Babylon and only a faithful remnant returned. The prophet Jeremiah promised that one day God would make a new covenant with his people. This time it would be written not on stone tablets but in the hearts of man. God said he would forgive their iniquity, and remember their sin no more. (See Jer. 31.)

## II. The Lord's Supper: the New Covenant Meal (1 Cor. 11)

Indeed, the prophecy of Jeremiah and others was fulfilled with the birth of Jesus the Messiah. The kingdom of God broke into human history and a new covenant was established with men. It was based not on birth and inheritance but on the new birth and faith. The meal which sealed and celebrates the new covenant is the Lord's Supper. Jesus said of it, "This cup is the new covenant in my blood" (1 Cor. 11:25).

The old covenant was ratified with the sacrifice of animals on the altar. The new covenant was ratified in the life's blood of Christ given on the cross.

The old covenant created a nation out of the nomadic children of Israel. They became the people of God. The new covenant created a "new Israel," the church, the new people of God.

The old covenant was based on obedience to the law of God, and the Israelites failed to be obedient. The new covenant is based on the grace of God and we appropriate it by faith.

Under the old covenant the children of Israel were delivered from slavery and human bondage. The new covenant results in God's delivering us from the bondage of sin and death.

There is a third Supper promised in the Bible:

### III. The Lamb's Supper in Heaven (Rev. 19)

The Lord's Supper will be observed in Christian worship "till he comes." Following the Lord's return all the redeemed of the ages will one day gather in the New Jerusalem. We will sit at table with the Lord at a great celebrative feast in heaven. What an honor that will be!

When you visit Windsor Castle outside London there are many impressive sights. One of the loveliest places is the royal dining room, with its great table. Here the knights of the British Order of the Garter gather to dine with the Queen. There is no higher honor in Great Britain. Think of it. One day we will dine with the King of kings and Lord of lords. Our faith relationship is one of sheer grace!

There are three great suppers in the Bible: the eating and drinking before the Lord on Mount Sinai which sealed the old covenant; the Lord's Supper as a symbol of our relationship in the new covenant; and that great banquet which awaits at the end of history in glory.

The Lord's Supper is a sign of the kingdom of God. Are you in the kingdom? Then welcome to the King's table. Let us break bread together.

## 8. What Mean These Stones?
Joshua 4:1-7,19-24, KJV

"He spake unto the children of Israel, saying, when your children shall ask their fathers in time to come, saying, What mean these stones?" (Josh. 4:21, KJV).

Man is a monument builder. The tourist is struck by this fact. After a two-week tour in Europe the cathedrals, castles, and monuments begin to blur in the memory. Civilization has spent millions on its monuments. Outside Cairo at Giza you see the pyramids and obelisks which were the glory of the Pharaohs. In Athens you visit the Parthenon built to honor the city's patron, the goddess Athena. In Rome you see the Colosseum, Forum, emperor's arches, and marble fountains. In Paris you drive around the Arc de Triomphe inaugurated by Napoleon. In London, Trafalgar Square is dominated by Wellington's monument and every roundabout seems to hold a statue. Washington, D.C., is a city of monuments and memorials to Washington, Jefferson, Lincoln, John F. Kennedy, and the Marines! Most every town in the southern United States has its Confederate memorial.

Why do we build such impressive monuments? Why has so much wealth been invested in this kind of effort across the centuries? There are many reasons.

We crave immortality and dread the thought of being forgotten. Visit a cemetery and reflect that despite all the monuments, simple and elaborate, we recognize few names more than one generation earlier than our own. The monument to the famous wartime prime minister in Westminster Abbey simply reads, "Remember Winston Churchill." There is something of the longing for immortality in that plaintive request.

We have poor memories, especially from one generation to the next. Persons and events vividly recalled by middle-aged adults may be a subject of complete ignorance among teenagers. A younger person may not consider it fashionable or "cool" to be interested in what concerns older people. We build our monuments "lest we forget."

We glorify great men and human achievements such as battles won, discoveries made, and leadership given. We want to remember our heritage, our roots, that from which we came and those who were before us.

The Hebrews memorialized the mighty acts of God. The scene depicted in Joshua 4 was an important one. It was the spring of the year, probably April, and the Jordan River was at flood stage. Melting snows from the mountains in Lebanon, including Mt. Hermon, overtaxed the river's narrow channel. On the east bank of the Jordan stood a multitude of motley nomads. They were former slaves from Egypt who had spent an entire generation living in the Sinai desert. Now they looked across the river toward the more highly civilized land of Canaan with anticipation. That Land of Promise had a much higher culture than the Hebrews who were about to invade it. These nomadic Israelites were going to come up against strong opposition. They were facing the walled cities of their enemies. However, they had one asset that was not so apparent: God was with them!

At the blare of rams horn trumpets the Hebrew priests, carrying the ark of the covenant swinging on poles, approached the waters of the swollen Jordan. Someone has suggested that suddenly there was a tremor, the shock of an earthquake. Some miles upstream clay cliffs sheared off and fell into the river, forming a temporary dam. "And when the soles of the feet of the priests who bear the ark of the LORD, the LORD of all the earth, shall rest in the waters of the Jordan, the waters of the Jordan shall be stopped from flowing, and the waters coming down from above shall stand in one heap" (Josh. 3:13). The Israelites viewed this event as a miracle of God, allowing them to walk across the bed of the Jordan River.

There was great rejoicing in the Israelite camp. A command was given and twelve large stones were piled up, as a memorial to God's intervention on behalf of his people. Notice that they viewed the crossing of the river, and later the conquest of Canaan, not as their achievement so much as God's mighty act on their behalf. They memorialized not their accomplishment, but God's gracious intervention. In a similar way, the Lord's Supper celebrates not our action, but God's action in our salvation.

One of the great values of monuments (and the Lord's Supper) is to arouse the curosity and interest of children. They would ask their fathers, "What mean these stones?" (v. 21) This would afford an opportunity to explain what God had done. Once at an observance of the Lord's Supper a young boy asked his father why we did that, and what did it mean? This inquiry gave the dad an opportunity to teach the child about what God has done for us in Christ. Such instruction should both provide information and call forth gratitude.

The Lord's Supper is a memorial which refreshes our memory about the central event in our salvation. It is a symbolic meal. The cup and loaf are not meant to feed us but to remind us of Christ and his sacrifice. The Lord's Supper is a celebration of God's intervention in human history on our behalf. We observe it together, in the divine presence.

"What mean these stones?" God dried up the Jordan and allowed the people to enter the Promised Land.

What mean these elements, this bread and cup? God gave us his Son and Christ gave his body and life's blood that we might be made the children of God.

Come, let us remember the Lord and his mighty acts for us—here at the Lord's table.

## 9. The Lord's Supper as Witness

"Every time you eat this loaf and drink the cup you are publicly proclaiming the Lord's death, until he comes again"(1 Cor. 11:26, Barclay).

The Lord's Supper is a form of preaching through the use of drama. The dramatic action of breaking, eating, and drinking carries the message (as does the act of immersion in baptism). As we eat this symbolic meal we sound the herald's trumpets. We are preaching by our action, Christ's victory on the cross over sin and death. We "show forth" the Lord's death.

We might come to church, see the table set for observance of the Lord's Supper, and think or say, "There will be no preaching today!" Don't you believe it. The observance of the ordinance can be one of the most powerful forms of preaching. Indeed, it can be preaching at its best, involving the congregation and using the spoken word, music, and vivid elements to proclaim eternal truth. Note 1 Corinthians 11:26: "For as often as you eat this bread and drink the cup, you proclaim [show forth, declare] the Lord's death until he comes." Thus, the ordinance is a powerful means of Christian proclamation. I have a friend who led his son to faith in Christ by discussing the meaning of the Lord's Supper.

Verbal preaching appeals to the ears and imagination. Proclamation through the Lord's Supper appeals to the eyes as well. By this dramatic action we preach to both the mind and the heart.

The Lord's Supper is

### I. A Witness to Christ

The bread is made from wheat which has been ground in the mill and baked in the oven. Even so the body of God's sinless Son was bruised, pierced, and broken for us on the cross.

The fruit of the vine is made from grapes crushed in the winepress. Even so our Lord poured out his life to secure our forgiveness and faith response. These are dramatic reminders of Christ and his sacrifice.

## II. A Witness to the Believer

This sacred Supper brings freshly to our minds the drama of the gospel: Jesus' matchless life, atoning death, and mighty resurrection. Our worship is far more than a wistful looking back to "days of yore." We are not recalling with nostalgia some golden age in the dim, dead past, when God in Christ walked the earth. We know that the risen Christ is here in our midst today in the Space Age. We might use the analogy of a good marriage. It is more than the memory of a beautiful ceremony or the ecstasy of a honeymoon, long ago. A meaningful marriage is helped by good memories, but its real joy is in the present, growing relationship of husband and wife. So the Supper has meaning for the participant.

## III. A Witness to the World

The Supper is a public proclamation. We have some reason to believe that the early church during times of persecution may have observed the Supper with no outsiders present. Sometimes the observance now days is held in the presence of only born-again believers who belong to a given congregation. However, the wording in 1 Corinthians 11:26 indicates clearly that the Supper has a messsage for the unsaved. Just as we do not strive to preach to the saved only, so I feel there is an evangelistic value in observing baptism and the Lord's Supper when the unsaved are present in the service. Many times they will come inquiring about the Lord, following a service in which they have seen one of the ordinances observed.

The Lord's Supper dramatically calls to the non-Christian: "Look, here is his body, here is his blood. They were given for you. It was for you he died!"

> We may not know, we cannot tell;
> What pains he had to bear;

But we believe it was for us
He hung and suffered there.

Christ's return will be a time of joy for believers, but a time of judgment for nonbelievers. We dare not neglect the evangelistic thrust of the Lord's Supper.

Which are you? Can you pray with sincerity and hope the one-word prayer of Revelation, *"Maranatha"*—come, Lord Jesus? If so, then take these elements with gratitude and joy. If not, then examine your heart, confess your need of the Savior, and receive him into your life just now. What time or place could be more appropriate? I invite you to respond, during the hymn of invitation.

## 10. The Power of a Great Example
John 13:1-17

The account of the institution of the Lord's Supper is found in the synoptic Gospels, Matthew, Mark, and Luke. It does not appear in the Fourth Gospel. However, John does give an account of Jesus washing the disciples' feet on the night of the first observance.

Jesus and his disciples gathered in the upper room to eat the Passover meal together. You will recall that the disciples entered that night arguing about which of them would be the greatest in the kingdom. They were not in a mood to be courteous, much less to worship.

There were few paved roads or streets in Palestine in New Testament times. It rains there only four months in the year and therefore it becomes very dusty. Men wore sandals. Before a meal a servant would wash the guests' feet. A basin of water and towel would have been provided, but none of the disciples offered to perform this menial task. Their pride was too great.

## I. Notice What Was in Jesus' Mind

John gives us three glimpses into the Master's thinking that night. First, he was aware that his hour had come. A number of times during Jesus' ministry he had refused to allow persons to force his hand, saying, "My hour has not yet come." Now the cross was imminent. Further, Jesus was keenly conscious of his mission. He knew that he had come from God and would return to God. He knew himself to be the Suffering Servant Messiah. His faith in God's purpose was firm, unfaltering. Finally, the Master was thinking of his disciples. He loved his own to the end, literally, to the uttermost. (And they were not very lovely at that moment.)

## II. Jesus' Enacted Parable

It was Jesus' strong self-confidence which enabled him to perform the lowly task. He arose, took off his outer robe, girded himself with a towel, and washed his disciples' dusty feet. The act was a vivid object lesson. Here was the greatest man who ever lived, performing a lowly servant's task.

The act had great symbolic meaning which we call to mind as we come to the Lord's table. It was an unforgettable lesson in humility. This was not a false humility like a great cook denying her gifts, or a brilliant man playing down the value of his intellect. Here was authentic humility. Just when Jesus was most keenly aware of his lordship, he could perform this lowly task. Nothing was beneath him. He was not "too good" to do this.

Jesus set an example for his disciples, then and now. He had said, "The Son of man came not to be served but to serve" (Matt. 20:28). He also said, "The servant is not above his lord" (John 13:16). Thus, he set the example for his servant church. Albert Schweitzer said that only those are happy who learn to serve. We serve by caring and helping to meet human need, including spiritual need.

Southern Baptist Missionary Parkes Marler served in South Korea working among 550 lepers. When he first went to this assignment, he was afraid of these diseased people. Many had lost their fingers, hands, ears, and noses. They were all disfigured by the leprosy.

However, he soon came to love them dearly. As he preached to them, a number became believers and were baptized. Missionary Marler told about hearing a Korean leper lady sing the gospel song "Where He Leads Me I Will Follow." Because part of her lips were gone the words sounded as though she was singing, "Where He *Needs* Me I Will Follow." That is the Christian's role and calling.

The Lord's Supper constitutes his call to care—and to serve. Jesus set the example. Will we follow?


## 11. Gethsemane and Beyond

"It is finished" (John 19:30).

At 3 P.M. one spring afternoon in the year A.D. 29 Jesus died on a cross on the skull-shaped hill of Golgotha, north of Jerusalem. His last word was *tetelestai*—it is finished! One afternoon not long before, back in Samaria, he had told his disciples, "My meat is to do the will of him that sent me, and to finish his work" (John 4:34, KJV). Now that great work of redemption was finished, "the great transaction done."

To see the significance of the cross-event more fully we must go back a few hours. We can gain perspective from the Mount of Olives and its small private garden called Gethsemane. There we learn that for Jesus his work was

### I. A Cup to Drink

"Let this cup pass from me" (Matt. 26:39) Jesus prayed. In Gethsemane there was the sound of the wind in the olive trees. There was the heavy breathing and snoring of the disciples as they slept in sheer exhaustion. From the south side of the garden came the sounds and the groans of a man in the agony of prayer.

The psalmist wrote about his cup running over, with gladness

(Ps. 23). But Jesus' cup was one of anguish and bitterness. It represented Jesus' chosen lot on our behalf. "All we like sheep have gone astray; we have turned every one to his own way; and the Lord hath laid on him the iniquity of us all" (Isa. 53:6, KJV).

The thought of crucifixion, its agony and infamy made Jesus shrink. He would have been less than a man if he had felt otherwise. Jesus' humanity is no place clearer seen than in Gethsemane. It was natural for him to dread that horrible experience and to pray that he might be spared it. There was more than the physical agony to be endured. Jesus also faced the desertion of his dearest friends, the mockery of the hostile crowd, and the wrath of God against sin. More than all this, the hardest part had to be when his heavenly Father looked away and Jesus was forsaken by God! Surely it was more than a man could stand. What a bitter cup! Yet Jesus drank it to the dregs that we might be saved.

Jesus' ministry and death was also

## II. A Road to Travel

"The Son of Man goeth as it is written of him" (Matt. 26:24).

Jesus' journey was a Via Dolorosa, a way of shame and suffering. He traveled it, bearing the sin of many. We may trace his route: the Messiah was promised and eagerly awaited for for centuries;

> he was born of Mary at Bethlehem;
> baptized by John in the Jordan River;
> he was tempted by Satan in the Judean wilderness;
> he taught, preached, and gave many signs of the
>     Kingdom in Galilee;
> he was acknowledged as Messiah by his disciples
>     at Caesarea Philippi;
> he journeyed to Jerusalem with its confrontation
>     with his enemies and a cross;
> he died in our place on the cross and was
>     raised from the dead by the power of God
>     on the first Easter morning.

What a journey! And now it is finished, completed, and he is at home with the Father in glory. The long and torturous road had a beautiful destination.

The life and death of Jesus was also

## III. A Price to Pay

Jesus said of himself, "The Son of man came not to be served but to serve, and to give his life a ransom for many" (Matt. 20:28).

Now the cross-event was no crass bargain between God and Satan. This is where the ransom theory of the atonement defies full explanation. Yet, in a way we cannot fully comprehend or explain, Jesus paid our sin debt on the cross. The price of sin is too high for us to pay. Jesus paid it all. The price we must pay is belief and commitment to our loving Lord.

Jesus summed up the meaning of his sacrifice when he said, "Greater love hath no man than this, that a man lay down his life for his friends" (John 15:13). Look again at these powerful metaphors of his atonement: a cup to drink, a road to travel, and a price to pay. All these are commemorated in our observance of the Lord's Supper.

A painting from World War I is intriguing. It portrays a scene in no-man's-land between the trenches. An Allied signal officer has gone out to repair a broken communications line. Just as he took hold of the ends of the wire, he was shot and killed. The artist pictured him lying there with the cable ends in his hands. The title of the painting is *Through*.

Sin severed communications between man and God, between heaven and earth. Christ, by his death on the cross, restored our communications and fellowship with our Creator. It cost him his life!

Thank God for Jesus Christ—the cup he drank, the road he traveled, and the price he paid, for us to be redeemed and restored. Let us thank him at the table.

Sidney Lanier wrote:

> Into the woods my Master went, Clean forspent, forspent;
> Into the woods my Master came, Forspent with love and shame.
> But the olives they were not blind to Him,
> The little gray leaves were kind to Him,
> The thorn tree had a mind to Him, When into the woods He came.

Out of the woods my Master went, And He was well content:
Out of the woods my Master came, Content with death and shame.
When death and shame would woo Him last,
From under the trees they drew Him last,
'Twas on a tree they slew Him last, When out of the woods He
    came.

Now, let us approach the table with a deeper awareness of its
meaning.

(As the elements are passed, let each recipient hand it to his fellow
believer and whisper, "Jesus said, 'This is my body' or 'This is
my blood.' "

At the conclusion of the observance, let the congregation join
hands and sing softly and without instrumental accompaniment the
hymn, "Blest Be the Tie." This final hymn may be the benediction.)

# 12. Symbol of Salvation
## Ephesians 1:3-7

"In whom we have redemption through his blood, the forgiveness
of sins, according to the riches of his grace" (Eph. 1:7, KJV).

I once heard a Bible translator tell about his search for a word
in an African dialect to translate the English word *redemption* or
*salvation*. Finally, an African working with the translator suggested
that he use the phrase, "he took our heads out." This strange phrase
had a rich significance for the people in that area. Captured slaves
used to be marched through that region en route to the coast and
slave ships. They wore iron collars with a chain going from the
neck of one slave to that of the one in front of him and behind
him. If you saw among the slaves a friend or relative, you could
pay the slave price and the master would unlock the iron collar,
take the man's neck out and set him free. "He took their heads

out." Not a bad way to express what God does in our redemption.
The Lord's Supper is a vivid symbol of our dearly bought freedom
in Christ.

Salvation history might be envisioned as something like an hour-
glass. At the top is the sand of all mankind. As you move down
the glass it narrows to the nation Israel, then to the faithful remnant,
and finally at the center to Christ alone. Then it begins to broaden
to the disciples, the 120 believers prior to the day of Pentecost,
then the early church, and now all authentic believers. The purpose
and goal of God is that all mankind and all creation might be saved.

Salvation originally meant to be spared from physical danger or
illness. When one narrowly escapes harm or death, we still speak
of his being "saved." Jesus saved the disciples from drowning when
they were caught in the storm on the Sea of Galilee. Obviously,
it is only a step to think of salvation as being applied to our deliverance from the penalty and tyranny of sin. We are told that Jesus
came to save his people from their sins. This salvation which begins
here will one day be complete at the end of history when Christ
comes again and establishes his dominion over all things.

Our salvation was purchased at an awesome cost by the death
of Christ on the cross.

> Jesus paid it all, all to him I owe;
> Sin had left a crimson stain,
> He washed it white as snow.

The Lord's Supper will not let us forget the great price that was
paid for our redemption.

Salvation is of God. He took the initiative for our redemption
by sending his Son. The Holy Spirit still takes the first step by
convicting us of our sins, convincing us of the Savior, and calling
us to believe. Repentance and belief is our response to God's grace.

This salvation is still available to all who repent and believe. It
is not our Father's will that any be lost. Once when William McKinley
was running for president of the United States he was traveling
through the Midwest by train. He had no plans to stop at a small
town in Illinois. The people requested that the train stop there and

the candidate make an appearance. McKinley's schedule was tight and word was sent to the small town that the campaign train could not stop. The townspeople were not to be outdone. They stretched "Old Glory" across the track, and dared the train to run over it. McKinley stopped and made a speech.

The Lord's Supper, as a symbol of salvation, is God's challenge, his barricade to stop us from going our way unheeding. God is pleading with us in the Supper. Will you hear him? Will you accept his offer of salvation? How do you answer his call?

## 13. Symbol of Sacrifice

For Christ has entered, not into a sanctuary made with hands, a copy of the true one, but into heaven itself, now to appear in the presence of God on our behalf. Nor was it to offer himself repeatedly, as the high priest enters the Holy Place yearly with blood not his own; for then he would have had to suffer repeatedly since the foundation of the world. But as it is, he has appeared once for all at the end of the age to put away sin by the sacrifice of himself (Heb. 9:24-26).

The Lord's Supper is like a fine diamond—it has many facets. Held in the light of Scripture, each reflects a brilliant truth.

The ordinance is a memorial: "This do in remembrance of me."

It is a proclamation: "You proclaim the Lord's death."

It is eschatological: "Till he comes."

It is a fellowship: "The communion of his body, the communion of his blood."

### I. The Supper Is Also a Symbol of Christ's Sacrifice

"This is my body . . . this is my blood." Isaiah wrote about the Suffering Servant, "He was oppressed, and he was afflicted, yet he opened not his mouth; like a lamb that is led to the slaughter, and like a sheep that before its shearers is dumb, so he opened not his mouth" (Isa. 53:7). John the Baptist identified Jesus as Messiah saying, "Behold, the Lamb of God, who takes away the sin of the world!" (John 1:29). In Revelation John wrote, "Worthy is the Lamb who was slain" (5:12).

By the end of the second century the church had come to call the Lord's Supper "the sacrifice." However, this concept was taken too far. The ordinance came to be viewed as a repenting of Christ's sacrifice. It was believed that his sacrifice was reenacted each time the "sacrament" was observed. Luther contended that this emphasis turned the gospel upside down. Calvary was the gift of God to man, and not the other way around. The author of Hebrews wrote that Christ was not offered repeatedly but "once for all." The Supper celebrates that one sufficient sacrifice.

## II. Why a Sacrifice? Why Was Such Required?

Sacrifice was God's way of dealing with our sin. "Without the shedding of blood there is no forgiveness" (Heb. 9:22). We tend to be casual about sin, to minimize it and laugh about it. We say it is common to man, or it's our business and no one else's. We forget the corporate nature of sin and its widening effects.

God takes sin far more seriously than we. He sent his only Son as the sacrifice to pay our sin debt. The suffering of the sinless Christ awakens our conscience to God's love and to the seriousness of our sin. The cross heightens our awareness of sin and calls forth gratitude at our forgiveness.

The Lord's Supper is a dramatic reminder of Christ's sacrifice, and the high cost of our redemption. There is no sense in which it is a reenactment of the cross. Rather, it points to the once-for-all, sufficient historical event. Christ's sacrifice is an accomplished fact, a finished work.

## III. Our Response

The sacrifice of Christ on our behalf calls forth our gratitude. Such a realization results in a faith response. "You are not your own. You have been bought, and at what a price!" (1 Cor. 6:19, Phillips). We, in turn, offer God our worship, ourselves. "I appeal to you therefore, brethren, by the mercies of God, to present your bodies as a living sacrifice, holy and acceptable to God, which is your spiritual worship. Do not be conformed to this world but be transformed by the renewal of your mind, that you may prove what is the will of God, what is good and acceptable and perfect" (Rom. 12:1-2).

We come now to the Lord's table, in gratitude for his sacrifice.

> Were the whole realm of nature mine,
>> That were a present far too small;
> Love so amazing, so divine,
>> Demands my soul, my life, my all.

# 14. Symbol of the Kingdom

The Lord's Supper is a foreshadowing of the messianic banquet in the kingdom of God. That will be a time of heavenly fellowship with the believers of the ages, with the Messiah, and with the Father.

## I. The Promise of the Banquet of God

First, Isaiah wrote to prophesy the time when God's people would feast in his presence: "On this mountain the Lord of Hosts will prepare a banquet of rich fare for all the peoples, a banquet of wines well matured and richest fare, well-matured wines strained clear. On this mountain the Lord will swallow up that veil that shrouds all the peoples, the pall thrown over all the nations; he will swallow up death for ever. Then the Lord God will wipe away the tears from every face and remove the reproach of his people from the whole earth. The Lord has spoken" (Isa. 25:6-8, NEB).

This bright prophecy looked forward to a new age when people from all nations will have fellowship with God, in festive celebration. Note that the occasion takes the form of an Oriental banquet. Man is made in the image of God—made to live in relationship with his Creator. He is also made for celebration. It appears that of all creatures, only man truly celebrates. Man has been called "Homo festivus."

Our celebration at the Lord's banquet will be so joyous and complete that sorrow and death will be banished. They will be no more. The Lord will wipe away all tears and forgive until all shame and guilt cease to exist. The apostle Paul had caught this vision. He wrote to Timothy, "Our Saviour Jesus Christ, who hath abolished death, and hath brought life and immortality to light through the gospel" (2 Tim. 1:10, KJV). He wrote to the early church in Greece, "Death is swallowed up in victory" (1 Cor. 15:54). Here is the glowing promise of life abundant with God in eternity. It has been anticipated for centuries and one day will come to fruition.

## II. Jesus Pictured the Kingdom as a Messianic Meal

In Matthew 8 we have the account of Jesus healing the Roman centurion's servant. Jesus was amazed at the soldier's faith. He had said to the Master, "Only say the word and my servant will be healed." Jesus commended the officer's faith and said, "I tell you, many will come from east and west and sit at table with Abraham, Isaac, and Jacob in the kingdom of heaven" (Matt. 8:11). Thus, Jesus envisioned the international and interracial character of the kingdom, and he saw it as a banquet.

One of the most vivid descriptions of the kingdom as a feast is found in Luke 14:

When one of those who sat at table with him heard this, he said to him, "Blessed is he who shall eat bread in the kingdom of God!" But he said to him, "A man once gave a great banquet, and invited many; and at the time for the banquet he sent his servant to say to those who had been invited, 'Come; for all is now ready.' But they all alike began to make excuses. The first said to him, 'I have bought a field, and I must go out and see it; I pray you, have me excused.' And another said, 'I have bought five yoke of oxen, and I go to examine them; I pray you, have me excused.' And another said, 'I have married a wife, and therefore I cannot come.' So the servant came and reported this to his master. Then the householder in anger said to his servant, 'Go out quickly to the streets and lanes of the city, and bring in the poor and maimed and blind and lame.' And the servant said, 'Sir, what you commanded has been done, and still there is room.' And the master said to the servant, 'Go out to the highways and hedges, and compel people to come in, that my house may be filled. For I tell you, none of those men who were invited shall taste my banquet' " (Luke 14:15-24).

Thus, we see that the kingdom of God and our faith is a thing of great joy. Indeed, we can say that joy is the essence of Christianity. Unhappy and joyless Christians are a contradiction. The ascetic spirit is out of step with the spirit of Jesus. Think about how many times the Gospel writers show us the Master at a meal, a banquet, a wedding party. Indeed, the word with which Jesus began each Beatitude (*mikarios*) is translated, "blessed, happy, O how happy, to be congratulated!"

The attitude of the Puritans and many Victorians was a misrepresentation of Jesus' attitude. One such church leader established a school for children with strict rules. For example, they were allowed to play no games. The idea prevalent at that time was, if he plays as a child, he will play as a man. There were no holidays from class. The children were required to rise at 4:00 A.M., spend an hour in prayer, and fast on Fridays until 3:00 P.M. Such regulations sound inhumane to moderns.

One of the Puritan theologians suffered from gallstones. Someone later remarked that there is little wonder his theological outlook was so pessimistic! The German philosopher Nietzsche taunted the dour evangelicals of his generation by saying they would have to look more redeemed if they wanted him to believe in their Redeemer. I once had a Scotchman on my church staff. When he first came to this country he was stunned that Baptists here read the Sunday edition of the newspaper. Consider the celebrative spirit of Jesus, by contrast. He was surely "Homo festivus."

### III. The Lord's Supper Anticipates the Heavenly Banquet

At the Supper's institution Jesus said, "I tell you I shall not drink again of this fruit of the vine until that day when I drink it new with you in my Father's kingdom" (Matt. 26:29). The word *day* may be capitalized for it is an eschatological reference to "the Day of the Lord." The Supper has a forward stance. It looks forward to the time when all the redeemed will sit at table with the Lord in heaven.

There are a number of Beatitudes in the book of Revelation. One of them speaks of this heavenly banquet: "Blessed are those who are invited to the marriage supper of the Lamb" (Rev. 19:9).

As persons in Christ, we are invited now to the Lord's table. One day we will join that host at the messianic banquet in heaven.

Come, let us celebrate the Lord's Supper. Hear these words of invitation:

> Come, not because you are strong, but because you are weak.
> Come, not because any goodness of your own gives you a right to come, but because you need mercy and help.
> Come, because you love the Lord a little and would like to love him more.
> Come, because he loved you and gave himself for you.
> Lift up your hearts and minds above your cares and fears and let this bread and wine be to you the token and pledge of the grace of the Lord Jesus Christ, the love of God and the fellowship of the Spirit, all meant for you if you will receive them in humble faith.
> I will take the cup of salvation and call upon the Lord.
> Blessed are they who hunger and thirst after righteousness for they shall be filled.
> O taste and see that God is good.[3]

## 15. Symbol of the Presence
Luke 24:13-35

"Then they told what had happened on the road, and how he was known to them in the breaking of the bread" (Luke 24:35).

That's what happened at Emmaus.

Where is God? Is he present here, on earth? The ancient Hebrews were quite sure God was on the earth. They spoke of him as the one who "dwelt in the bush" (Deut. 33:16), referring to the call of Moses from the burning bush. They also spoke of God as the one who "dwells between the cherubim" (1 Sam. 4:4). The ark of the covenant in the tabernacle had a pair of cherubim on top of it. They faced each other and their wing tips touched overhead. Beneath their wing tips was the mercy seat—the dwelling place of God on earth. In later Hebrew history Solomon built a Temple for God on Mount Moriah in Jerusalem. It was considered a house in which God's presence dwelt—in the holy of holies.

Modern persons may consider the Hebrew concepts of God dwelling on earth, in a bush, on a box, in a building, as primitive. However, despite our supposed sophistication we, too, think of God in terms of the places where we have encountered him. We have our sacred spots as well, where God has been real in our experience. The danger in this is that we may tend to limit God to the places where we met him, or to our nation or denomination. This was Jonah's problem. He thought of the Lord as a local deity and tried to escape his presence and call. As we all know, Jonah was terribly mistaken in trying to limit God.

God was certainly on the earth in Christ. His name was Immanuel, which means "God with us." The Scriptures tell us that "God was in Christ reconciling the world to himself" (2 Cor. 5:19).

Where on earth is God today?

## I. God Is Omnipresent—Present Every Place

He is not simply the God of Israel or America. He is the God of all nations and the entire universe. There is no time or place where God is absent. Recall how the psalmist concluded that there was no place where he could go and escape the divine presence.

God stands in a special relationship to the world. "The earth is the Lord's." He created it and sustains it by his providential power. Further, he is bringing the world to his predetermined end and goal. The earth is no accident and its future no mystery. "This is my Father's world."

Wherever we are, God is near and anxious to be our loving Father. He is the God of the now. He revealed his name to Moses as "I AM," not "I Was" or "the Great Has-Been." He is not embalmed someplace in ancient history. He is God of the Space Age and is hardly amused at our nuclear firecrackers.

## II. God Is with Believers in a Special Way

He stands in a very special relationship to his "New Creation." Jesus said, "Where two or three are gathered in my name, there am I in the midst of them" (Matt. 18:20). That text is not a consolation prize for a small church attendance. It is a Hebrew idiom for a group. And more than that, it is a promise of the divine Presence! Even as we observe the Lord's Supper today, the service is being broadcast and deacons have gone to many homes and nursing homes. They have taken the elements with them and as we take the bread, they take the bread. As we take the cup in remembrance of him, they will take the cup, too. They are worshiping along with us, though they are not physically present in the church building. And the risen Christ is with us all. This morning we are an extended congregation, and Christ is with and within all believers.

The apostle Paul described believers as being persons "in Christ." This is one of the major terms in his New Testament epistles. He wrote about our bodies being the temple of the Holy Spirit and concluded: "Christ in you, the hope of glory" (Col. 1:27).

Brother Lawrence spoke about "practicing the presence of God."

He was an humble believer who spent most of his time working in a kitchen. And yet he was aware of being in the divine Presence.

### III. There Are Times When God Is Especially Near

We become aware of his focused Presence in times which Elton Trueblood calls the "common ventures of life." These include such times as conversion, marriage, the birth of a child, and bereavement. We might add high moments of worship, including baptism and observance of the Lord's Supper.

Greek has two words for "time." One is *chronos* from which we get the English word *chronology*. It means measured time, by clock or calendar. The other word is *kairos* which means intense or filled time. The times when we are keenly aware of God's presence are *kairos* times.

Just as God was incarnate in Jesus, so he is present in the risen Christ in our worship. He is not present in any magical or mechanical sense. But he is mystically and symbolically present with us. Jesus promised, "Lo, I am with you always, even to the end of the age."

Come, let us worship him as we take the elements which symbolize his presence.

Prayer by Richard of Chichester:

> These three things we pray, Grant we may
>   see Thee more clearly;
>   love Thee more dearly;
>   follow Thee more nearly. Amen.

# 16. Symbol of the Covenant

He [Moses] took the book of the covenant, and read in the audience of the people: and they said, "All that the LORD hath said we do, and be obedient" (Ex. 24:7, KJV).

Behold, the days come, saith the LORD, that I will make a new covenant with the house of Israel, and with the house of Judah . . . . But this shall be the covenant that I will make with the house of Israel; After those days, saith the Lord, I will put my law in their inward parts, and write it in their hearts; and will be their God, and they shall be my people. And they shall teach no more every man his neighbour, and every man his brother, saying, Know the LORD; for they shall all know me, from the least of them unto the greatest of them, saith the LORD: for I will forgive their iniquity, and I will remember their sin no more (Jer. 31:31-34, KJV).

From start to finish, from Genesis 17 to Revelation 21 one of the great motif's of the Bible is the idea of a covenant. It occurs 286 times in the Old Testament Scriptures alone! Indeed, we call the Bible the Old and New Testaments which means the old and new covenants. If some Christian groups have given this idea too much attention, we Baptists have probably given it too little.

## I. The Old Covenant

Simply stated, a covenant is an agreement or contract between two persons or parties. When we sign a binder on a house, we covenant to buy it. When we exchange vows and rings in our wedding, we "covenant together" in matrimony. When nations ratify treaties, they are often called covenants. Entering into a covenant is almost always a time for great joy (and perhaps a little anxiety).

God made a covenant with Abraham (read Gen. 17). God took the initiative and chose Abraham. He called him to follow in faith. God promised to bless Abraham and make of his descendents a holy nation. God promised that through Abraham all mankind would be blessed. That came to pass with the birth of Christ. In return, Abraham was required to be faithful and obedient to God. He became the man of faith par excellence.

Later at Mount Sinai God cut a covenant with Abraham's descendants. Notice the pattern of that covenant:

The preamble, "I am the LORD your God, who brought you out of the land of Egypt, out of the the house of bondage (Ex. 20:2).

The stipulations of the covenant are the Ten Commandments.

The covenant was written and read publicly.

Blessings were pronounced for their obedience to the covenant, and curses for their disobedience. (See Ex. 20.)

Over the years Israel failed to be obedient to the Law of God and to share their faith as he intended. Therefore, Jeremiah promised that one day God would make a new covenant. Centuries later that prophecy was fulfilled in the upper room when Jesus said, "This is my blood of the covenant" (Matt. 26:28).

## II. The New Covenant

It, too, was initiated by God when he sent his Son into the world. "For God so loved the world, that he gave his only begotten Son, that whosoever believeth in him should not perish, but have everlasting life" (John 3:16, KJV). Therefore, we love him because he first loved us and gave himself up for us. This covenant, like the old, is not an agreement between equal parties. God is the "Senior Partner." This new covenant, too, is conditional upon our faith and obedience. We are to carry out the mission he has given us, and share our faith. The covenant and grace require it.

The Supper also symbolizes our new fellowship with other believers. We are reminded that we belong to a blood-bought fraternity. The closer we come to God the nearer we approach our fellow believers. The more we love God, the more we come to love the brethren. In John Masefield's *The Everlasting Mercy*, the character Saul Kane declares at his conversion:

> I did not think, I did not strive,
> The deep peace burnt my me alive;
> The bolted door had broken in,
> I knew that I had done with sin.
> I knew that Christ had given me birth
> To brother all the souls on earth.[4]

We share a common faith symbolized in this common meal.

Obedience to the covenant issues in joy, for as we are obedient we please God. The new covenant makes us the people of God, a holy nation, a royal priesthood. God is glorified as we share the knowledge of him with others. The covenant is a matter of God's gracious choice. We do not deserve it and cannot earn it.

The Lord's Supper is a powerful symbol of our new covenant

relationship with God. Let us approach his table, aware that we are here entering into relationship with the eternal.

## 17. The Lord's Supper—and Ours

"The cup of blessing which we bless, is it not a participation in the blood of Christ? The bread which we brake, is it not a participation in the blood of Christ? Because there is one bread, we who are many are one body, for we all partake of the one loaf" (1 Cor. 10:16-17).

The Lord's Supper is a very simple observance with a crystal clear meaning. However, across the centuries the church has made it an elaborate and ornate ritual. We have clothed it in mystery and obscured its simple message. It is really concerned with the consecration of the common place. Jesus instituted this memorial meal using ordinary everyday items: bread and wine. Had he begun the ordinance in our time, he might have used coffee and doughnuts or coke and cookies. These were the two items of food which would have been found in even the homes of the poor in Jesus' day. Bread has been the staff of life for some seven thousand years, since the days of the earliest human settlements. The fruit of the vine has been a common beverage since ancient times.

In the Lord's Supper Jesus took these ordinary elements and gave them a symbolic meaning. He said they stood for his body and his blood.

### I. The Lord's Supper

This is the Supper of the Master. All who know, love, and faithfully follow Christ come to worship him here at the table. There is a vertical dimension to our communion. Here we meet the Master and have fellowship with him.

How can sinful persons approach a holy God? Our sin short-circuits our communication and fellowship with him. It is a barrier which separates us from our Maker. Therefore, God took the first step to establish a relationship with us, to open up communication. That first step was the incarnation—he sent his Son.

The New Testament simply piles up terms and metaphors to describe this gospel truth. One such word is drawn from the law courts. In Christ, God *pardons* our offense and acquits us of our sin.

Another image is taken from the slave market. It is hard for us to realize that half the population in the Greco-Roman world were slaves. In Christ, God *ransomed* us, bought us back, paying our sin debt in full. The New Testament describes our salvation by saying that God in Christ has bought us. "You have been bought, and at what a price! Therefore bring glory to God in your body" (1 Cor. 6:19-20, Phillips).

The Lord's table reminds us of the Lord and our redemption.

## II. Our Supper

Jesus said, "This is for you." It was for you he died, on Calvary, and therefore, there is a sense in which this is the believer's table. The Lord's Supper is not a solitary or private affair. It is a church ordinance which we observe corporately. The Supper has a horizontal dimension. At the table we relate to one another, as well as to the Lord. In August 1946, as a boy, I saw an observance of the Lord's Supper which greatly impressed me. Four generations of my family had worshiped at a small church which had been established following the Civil War. My great-grandfather, James Hubbard McEachern, was one of its charter members. They had worship only on fourth Sundays, though there was a weekly Sunday School for a time. In the spring of that year my great-grandfather, in his ninetieth year, was struck by an automobile, walking from work. (He was manager of a cotton warehouse.) His hip was broken, and he spent the last six months of his life at home in bed.

On the fourth Sunday in August the church met for worship. They adjourned the service and all came to my great-grandfather's home.

Gathered in his sickroom, the hallway, and adjoining rooms, they observed the Lord's Supper. Afterward, he told me with tears how meaningful that worship service had been to him. On September 3, my fourteenth birthday, he died. The Supper is the Lord's; yet it is something we observe along with other believers.

As we approach the Lord's table, and ours, let us first examine ourselves. This is a time for confession. We confess our sins of habit, attitude, and negligence. We have failed to help and encourage, to care and witness. Let us ask the Father's forgiveness.

It is also a time to confess our faith and our love for God and one another. Now, let us take the Supper, with gladness and great joy.

## 18. Where We Meet God

The purpose of God for all creation is that it be brought under the lordship of Christ. In him the fullness of deity dwelled bodily.

> He is the image of the invisible God, the first-born of all creation; for in him all things were created, in heaven and on earth, visible and invisible, whether thrones or dominions or principalities or authorities—all things were created through him and for him. He is before all things, and in him all things hold together. He is the head of the body, the church; he is the beginning, the first-born from the dead, that in everything he might be pre-eminent. For in him all the fulness of God was pleased to dwell, and through him to reconcile to himself all things, whether on earth or in heaven, making peace by the blood of his cross (Col. 1:15-20).

We were made in the image of God, made for fellowship with him. By faith in Christ we are at one with him: "Christ in you, the hope of glory" (v. 27). Since we are made for fellowship with our heavenly Father, we encounter him in various ways.

How and where do we encounter God? How and where does he disclose himself to us? The Scriptures contain the record of many persons who met God in days past. Abraham was the friend of God who lived in a covenant relationship with his Creator. God was real in the experience of the Old Testament prophets and others. With the birth of Jesus, God came into his world. His name was Immanuel—God with us! God walked the dusty streets of Palestine in the person of his Son, Jesus.

However, the question is not simply did it happen in the eighth century B.C. and in A.D. 29, but does it happen today? Does God still encounter us in this generation? If so, how and where does this occur?

## I. We May Encounter God in Our Mothers' Laps

That is where I first learned the name of Jesus and felt the love of God. It is hardly possible to overemphasize the importance of our early spiritual influences. Parents, grandparents, other relatives, and teachers made profound impressions on us for good or ill. In our religious education program we need our most skilled and dedicated teachers working with young children. Think back to your childhood and recall those who influenced your life for good and for God. If some of these persons are alive, resolve to express your appreciation for them. A visit, phone call, or note to them can be a great encouragement. Many of us can say we first encountered God in a Christian home.

## II. We Can Encounter God in Crisis Times

Someone indicated that the Chinese word for crisis has the same characters as the word *opportunity*. It is true that a crisis experience can be an opportunity to encounter God. This is not always the case. Crisis times may cause us to become bitter and blame God.

The common ventures in life can cause us to be aware of the nearness of God. At such times the veil separating this earthly life from the spiritual reality all about us seems thin. One such spiritual crisis is conversion. For many this occurs around the age of ten or twelve. With a child's faith, we affirm our love for God and our faith in Christ. Whenever conversion occurs, it is a spiritual crisis of eternal dimensions.

Another crisis may occur during adolesence. It can center in the choice of our life's work, or the answering of God's call. Sometimes it occurs at a summer assembly or retreat. We often refer to such times as "a mountaintop experience," recalling the transfiguration. What is at stake in this experience is the lordship of Christ in our lives. It may be that we are quite willing for him to be Savior but unsure about letting him be Lord of our life. This is especially true when it appears that his will for our life may be in conflict with what we want to do. We may encounter God, rather uncomfortably. This experience often results in a rededication of our life to him.

There are many milestones at which God becomes especially real to us. These can include such experiences as entering college or military service, beginning a career or profession, the time of marriage, the birth of a child, retirement, or bereavement. These common ventures all involve risks and all have the potential for human-divine encounter.

C. S. Lewis said that God whispers in our pleasures, speaks in our joys, shouts in our pain. Pain is God's megaphone to rouse a listless world.

While God may disclose himself in the crisis or high hours, never forget that

## III. We Can Encounter God in the Ordinary

How do we recognize the great moments when they come in the midst of the ordinary routine? God is sovereign. The Holy Spirit, like the wind, blows where it will. There is a holy unpredictability about the One with whom we have to do.

Since God made the world and made us, we may encounter him anyplace and at any time. Maltbie D. Babcock expressed this in the words of this hymn:

> This is my Father's world, And to my list'ning ears,
> All nature sings, and round me rings
>   The music of the spheres.
> This is my Father's world, I rest me in the thought

Of rocks and trees, of skies and seas;
His hand the wonders wrought.

This is my Father's world, The birds their carols raise;
The morning light, the lily white
Declare their Maker's praise.
This is my Father's world, He shines in all that's fair;
In the rustling grass I hear him pass, He speaks to me
ev'rywhere.

We may very well encounter God in one whom we help; in a child's smile or candid remark; in love's embrace. We might as well come to expect him in the unexpected.

## IV. We Can Encounter God at the Table

Worship comes from an old Anglo-Saxon word, worth-ship. The purpose of our worship is to ascribe supreme worth to God. Praise and adoration is at the heart of our worship. Surely, all believers can recall moments when the transcendent came near. It may have been in a service of public worship, family, or private devotions. Many of us would give a testimony to the growing value and meaning of the Lord's Supper observance in our spiritual life.

The presence of God is in all the world, and all persons are his children by creation. Yet there is a sense in which his presence is focused for us in Christian worship, and believers are his children by both creation and redemption.

Here at the Lord's table we may meet him, experience his forgiveness, and feel his claim on us. Here the glories of the Scripture and twenty centuries of Christian history can come alive for us. The God who commissioned the apostle Paul, converted Augustine, and warmed the heart of John Wesley may do it again where we are—in our lives. God keeps breaking into human history, even in our worship.

The Lord's Supper is not simply a remembrance of past encounter. The risen Christ is here in his Word read and proclaimed; here at his table. Just as surely as the early disciples met him beside the sea, in the marketplace, on the grassy hillside—so may we meet him here and now.

The question is: Are you alert to his presence? Are you open to encounter his Spirit? Are you listening for a word from beyond? Do you really expect to meet the Master as you take the bread and cup? You don't have to meet him. There is nothing automatic about it. But you may!

When we meet God, we become intensely aware of his person and presence. We also become aware of our inadequacy and sinfulness. Such an encounter creates the necessity of decision and choice. When we confront God we also become aware of others, their uniqueness and their need.

You can encounter Christ here.

# 19. Symbol of Self-Examination

The Scots' nickname for Edinburgh, their capital, is "Auld Reekie." We would translate it into English as "Old Smoky." Since the Industrial Revolution, it has been a smoky city except on the sabbath day when the air clears and you can see "forever."

The Lord's Supper is a place where theological clouds part, and we come back to basics. This is no place for philosophical speculation or psychological self-analysis. This is a place for worship. We can take our shoes off for the ground on which we stand is holy. This is a time when things come clear, for Christ is here.

## I. The Bread and Cup of Thanksgiving

He took the cup and gave thanks. Eucharist or thanksgiving is one of the names for the Lord's Supper.

Be thankful for God's provision. He has provided our food. Did you have enough to eat during the holidays? Most of us had too much. Have you ever thought how wonderful it is to know your drinking water is safe? There are many places in the world where it is not.

God has provided us with this free land. On April 15, when you pay your taxes, you may think it's not so free, but we do enjoy freedom in self-government. We can turn the rascals out. We live in a land that knows justice and due process of law. America is a land of opportunity where a man can get an education and earn a living and advance himself and his family.

God has provided the Savior to forgive our sins and make us children of the King. He has given us God the Holy Spirit to empower us every day of this new year. He has given us the Bible as our guidebook and prayer as the means of communication with himself. He has given the church to nurture us and to bring us up in its sweet fellowship. Pardon my prejudice—thank God for our church and the great fellowship we have here.

"He took the cup and gave thanks."

## II. "Let a Man Examine Himself"

Let us confess our sins to God. Let us confess the wrong actions we have taken during the past year. We have been selfish and indulgent. We have been clannish and narrow in our sympathies. Remember, Jesus said that if we love only those that love us, we are no better than the pagans. There is honor even among thieves. The Christian is to go the second mile. He is expected to do more than is required. We have hurt others, and the chief sin of all is that we have been uncaring.

Let us confess our wrong attitudes. We have a false sense of superiority. We feel that we are better than other people. We are guilty of the pride of intellect, achievement, and race. Let us confess our prejudice for we despise those who are different.

Let us confess our sins of neglect. We have failed to express gratitude and to be considerate. We have failed to encourage others. We have failed to witness to lost relatives and friends and to be Christlike in all our attitudes.

At the Lord's Supper, we also take courage. Are you perplexed? Then, let me remind you that Jesus said, "I am the way, the truth, and the life" (John 14:6). Do you feel guilty? Then remember the verse which says, "If we confess our sins, he is faithful and just, and will forgive our sins and cleanse us from all unrighteousness" (1 John 1:9). Are you troubled? Then hear the Scripture, "[Cast] all your care upon him, for he careth for you" (1 Pet. 5:7, KJV). Are you burdened? Hear Jesus: "Come unto me, all ye that labour and are heavy laden, and I will give you rest. Take my yoke upon you" (Matt. 11:28, KJV). Are you bored with life—"As my Father hath sent me, even so send I you" (John 20:21, KJV). You have a mission and a ministry. There are some today who are bereaved by the loss of loved ones. Hear the words of Jesus, "I will not leave you comfortless: I will come to you" (John 14:18, KJV).

### III. The Lord's Table Is a Reminder of Our Salvation

When we who are saved look at it, we recognize the great cost of our salvation. We are not our own—we are bought at a price—and what a price!

To the unsaved this table is an opportunity as clear as the spread table. The Lord's Supper constitutes Christ's call to you to salvation. Don't go away without him.

In a way which I cannot explain or fully understand, Christ is really present here at his table, not magically or mechanically but mystically. Your faith can make his presence real to you or your unfaith can make his presence null and void.

I was driving up a hill once in West Virginia when I came upon a Lutheran church. In front of it was a huge cross. At the top were the words in Latin, Hebrew, and Greek: "Jesus of Nazareth, King of the Jews." At the foot of the cross was this question: "Is it nothing to you, all ye who pass by?" The Lord's table represents his presence and our salvation. Is it nothing to you?

## 20. "Lord, Is It I?"
Matthew 26:20-30

Our observance of the Lord's Supper is an opportunity to experience the divine presence in our worship. Such an encounter will call us to a sense of awe and wonder: "Holy, holy, holy is the Lord God of Hosts!" As we draw near to his table we become aware of God. However, our worship which focuses on him also reflects on ourselves. It calls for seeing oneself as God sees us.

Note Matthew's prelude to the institution of the Supper. It was Thursday of Jesus' last week on earth prior to his crucifixion. He had sent Peter and John to make preparation for the disciple band to eat the Passover meal together. Meanwhile, Jesus must have said farewell to Lazarus, Mary, and Martha at Bethany and made the short journey to Jerusalem. He would have climbed the outdoor stairway to the roof of the house and its large upper room. This guest room contained a large table set for the thirteen men who would eat the commemorative meal there. On the table were the traditional ingredients of a Passover meal: roasted lamb, unleavened bread, cups of wine, bitter herbs, salt water, and so forth.

Light from the olive oil lamps cast a soft glow over the men who had entered the room quarreling about which of them would be greatest in the kingdom. Jesus had taught them humility with a water basin and towel by washing their dusty feet. Perhaps they ate the meal of remembrance, celebrating the Exodus in near silence. Then in his discourse Jesus said to the group, "One of you shall betray me." The startled group responded asking, "Lord, is it I?"

That intriguing question is appropriate for us.

We know there is evil within our own hearts. To ask, "Is it I?" is to acknowledge the possibility of evil in every heart. Not one of the disciples accused another. They knew in all candor and honesty that any one of them might be capable of betraying the Master.

Thus, we see evil brought home. When we hear of another's fault, we realize that it could have been us. When we are tempted, we know that the tempter's appeal may very well strike an answering chord in the depths of our own desire. You may recall that in the account of Cain and Abel, God said to Cain, "Sin lieth at the door." The Hebrew word is one used to describe a crouching animal ready to pounce and destroy. Temptation is not something to be toyed with, not something to be entertained and cuddled. We are told in the Scriptures that we are to "resist the devil" and that we are to "call on the name of the Lord" in order that we might be saved from the tempter's power.

The disciples' question, "Is it I?" also demonstrates the fact that we really don't know ourselves. Could I be the one to betray Jesus, they were asking. Is this terrible evil lurking within me? No man falls suddenly. Bad character is not formed in a moment. The Scripture describes the betrayer in these terms: "Judas, who *became* a traitor" (Luke 6:16). He did not start out to be one. That was not his original intention. In fact, earlier, he would have been startled if anyone had said he had the capacity to betray the Master.

Just as surely as we do not fall suddenly, or that is seldom the case, so there are also warnings that come to us if we are perceptive. We may be warned by a dim voice of conscience when we are alone. A warning may come in the form of the death of a loved one or a friend, or it may take the guise of a personal illness or a narrow escape from harm. We may be warned by the noble example of some fine person or by the fall of another whom we have known.

Surely, we can be warned of the tempter's power in our worship and meditation and prayer. Jesus said, "One of you will betray me." That very phrase constituted a word of warning and note of appeal to the one who would betray him.

We are told by the apostle Paul that the observance of the Lord's Supper is to be preceded by a man's examining himself. The psalmist sang, "Search me, O God, and know my heart." The Lord's table is a place where we are to ask and receive divine forgiveness. Such forgiveness grows out of the sheer grace of God. Jesus said to the woman taken in adultery, "Go and sin no more" (KJV). Here in the fellowship of other believers we find at the communion table grace to make us equal to the testing time. Indeed, each of the disciples had a tremendous spiritual potential, far beyond what they may have imagined that night. They not only had a potential for betrayal, but also one for heroic witness. Peter, who sat at the table with Jesus, would deny his Lord, but he would also be restored and become the chief among the apostles. John was faithful even to the point of being banished to the Isle of Patmos, and it was through his vision of the church triumphant that we get a glimpse of glory. According to tradition, every one of the disciples met with martydom with the exception of John. Here at the table, let us recognize our potential for denial and betrayal but also our potential for doing great things for God.

We recognize that we, too, could be a traitor. Let us echo the disciples' question, "Lord, is it I?" and repeat the prayer he taught us to pray, "Lead us not into temptation [bring us not to the test], but deliver us from evil" (Matt. 6:13). Now, let us worship him as we take the elements of remembrance.

## 21. Symbol of His Body

Jesus said, "This is my body, which is for you" (1 Cor. 11:24).

Even though this is the oldest document in the New Testament and the earliest account of the Lord's Supper in the Scriptures, it was not original with Paul. He wrote, "I have received" this account. It was an earlier tradition handed on to Paul by others in the early church. Doubtless, Paul got the story from some of Jesus' disciples who were with him that night when he instituted the ordinance. In the later accounts in the Synoptic Gospels Jesus is reported as having said, "This is my body." The author of the Fourth Gospel wrote, "He who eats my flesh and drinks my blood has eternal life, and I will raise him up at the last day" (John 6:54).

## I. Consider the Incarnate Christ

We believe that God became a man in the person and flesh of Jesus of Nazareth. Mysteriously he was both human and divine, both man and God. This does not mean that he was some sort of demigod, half man and half god, like some character in Greek mythology. He was fully human and fully God at the same time and in the same person. John's Gospel and Epistles state this truth clearly:

> In the beginning was the Word, and the Word was with god, and the Word was God. He was in the beginning with God; all things were made through him, and without him was not anything made that was made. In him was life, and the life was the light of men. The light shines in the darkness, and the darkness has not overcome it (John 1:1-5).

And "The Word became flesh [a human being, TEV] and dwelt among us, full of grace and truth; we have beheld his glory, glory as of the only Son from the Father" (v. 14). The writer of 1 John wrote about Jesus as an eyewitness. "That which was from the beginning, which we have heard, which we have seen with our eyes, which we have looked upon and touched with our hands . . . we proclaim to you" (1 John 1:1-2). We know that the body of Jesus was actually that of God in human flesh. The great miracles of our faith are the incarnation and the resurrection.

Jesus chose bread as a symbol of his body. Consider its brokenness: You break the ground to plant wheat. The wheat is cut and beaten with a flail to extract the grain. Then it is crushed and ground to make flour. Flour and water or milk are mixed and then baked in an oven to make bread. Finally, the bread is broken at the table in order to be eaten. What a vivid symbol of his body given and broken for our salvation. This very thing happened to Jesus on the cross. That night when Jesus said, "This is my body," he was giving a prophecy of what was to happen within a few hours. We look back at that event with deepest gratitude.

## II. The Body of Christ Today

There are two distinct ways in which we may think of the body of Christ today. The risen Christ has a glorified body since his resurrection. It seems mysterious to us. It was real, for he spoke with his disciples, he ate with them, and they could see his wounds and touch him. Yet, he could come and go at will. He could enter a locked room and then disappear. His new body was fitted for a different realm and existence from our own world. We get excited when we think of his glorified body because Christ is the firstfruits of the resurrection. One day we, too, will have a new body like his. One day we, too, will be "clothed on with immortality."

Jesus ascended fifty days after his resurrection. His glorified body is now in heaven, at the right hand of God's throne (the position of highest honor). There he is exalted and makes intercession for us. At his martyrdom, deacon Stephen saw the risen Christ in a vision. As he was being stoned he said, "Behold, I see the heavens opened, and the Son of man standing at the right hand of God" (Acts 7:56).

There is another sense in which the New Testament speaks of the body of Christ. The church is his corporate body. "We who are many are one body" (1 Cor. 10:17). Paul also wrote concerning the church: "There is one body and one Spirit, just as you were called to the one hope . . . one Lord, one faith, one baptism, one God and Father of us all, who is above all and through all and in all" (Eph. 4:4-6). The body of Christ is the church. It is made up of millions and yet we are one. The church consists of all believers of all time. It includes the church triumphant—all believers in heaven, and the church militant—all believers on earth. There is also a sense in which the church has yet to include all persons who are predestined to believe on Christ, including those not yet born. The church is the body of Christ and he is its head.

## III. Our Bodies

Just as Christ spoke of the bread as symbolic of his body, the Scripture speaks about the importance of our human bodies. "I appeal to you therefore, brethren, by the mercies of God, to present your bodies as a living sacrifice, holy and acceptable to God, which is your spiritual worship" (Rom. 12:1).

One day, we, too, will receive an immortal body. Hebrew theology never conceived of a man less his body, as complete. Therefore, we believe in a bodily resurrection of the dead and a bodily return of Christ. First Corinthians 15 is the greatest chapter in the Bible on the resurrection body. This is not some crass doctrine of the resuscitation of human corpses. It does not imply that this mortal flesh will have its molecules reassembled and its life revived. No, the human body is buried mortal to be raised immortal at the last day. It will become a transformed and glorified body, like that of the risen Christ. His resurrection is the basis of our immortality. This is the miracle par excellence and the foundation of our faith.

Jesus said of the broken bread, "This is my body." Let us eat it with thanksgiving and gratitude—in remembrance of him.

## 22. Symbol of His Blood

Jesus said, "For this is my blood of the covenant, which is poured out for many for the forgiveness of sins" (Matt. 26:28).

The New Testament writers placed great importance on the symbol of the blood of Christ. You see his blood represented his life given freely for us. John wrote, "The blood of Jesus his son cleanses us from all sin" (1 John 1:7). Paul could say, "Having made peace through the blood of his cross" (Col. 1:20 KJV) and "In him we have redemption through his blood" (Eph. 1:7).

Some people relate almost superstitiously to the idea of the blood of Christ (and the cup which symbolizes it). They may believe that a miracle occurs when the cup is consecrated, so that the wine becomes the actual blood of Christ. Or they may make the words "the blood of Christ" an essential catch word or code of orthodoxy. Once after a worship service a visitor said to me, "That was a good sermon, but there was no mention of the blood."

Others are repelled at the idea and mention of the blood of Christ. They consider the term offensive and may say, "I'll have no part in such a gory religion. It's simply impolite to mention such in public." But how can we ignore such a central theme in both the Old and New Testaments? The author of Hebrews went so far as to write, "Without shedding of blood is no remission" (9:22, KJV).

Remember that in biblical theology the life is in the blood. In Old Testament sacrifice an animal was killed. Parts of it were burned and the flesh was cooked and eaten by the worshipers and priests. But the blood of the animal, which represented its life, was offered on the altar to God. Even so, on the cross Christ's blood was poured out as the perfect offering to God for our sins. To speak of Christ's blood is to speak of his life given.

The observance of the Lord's Supper brings us to the central support of our faith. One summer I visited the magnificent cathedral of Notre Dame in Paris. This site has been a place of worship for centuries, even before Christianity. I wanted to make a picture of the great church, but the sun was not right for me to photograph the towers and entrances. So, I went around to the back. From that view the flying buttresses were visible. These stone arches soar high in the air and turn to support the upper walls of the nave. The ordinances are the flying buttresses of our faith. They soar to support the lofty truths which point us toward God.

Baptism is the initiation rite into the church. In our baptism we declare our faith in Christ. The Lord's Supper is the rite of remembrance by which we renew and redeclare our faith periodically.

## I. The Lord's Supper Is Historical—It Points to the Cross

It symbolizes and brings vividly to mind Christ's sacrifice outside Jerusalem in A.D. 29. It brings us back to center, reminding us of our need as sinners and God's gracious provision for our forgiveness. Man's greatest need is not material things. Someone said that a rich man and a poor man have one thing in common—neither knows how much it would take to make him happy! Our greatest need is not more knowledge, as important as that is. To be reminded of how dangerous an educated pagan and criminal can be we only have to remember the Nazis. Our greatest need is spiritual—to be rightly related to God. We cannot be right with our fellowmen until we are first right with our Maker. Humanism starts at the wrong end. The Lord's Supper points the way to God, and then it underlines our fellowship with others.

## II. The Lord's Supper Is Mystical—It Points to the Risen Christ

Obviously, the Supper has a significance greater than itself, just as the nation's flag is more than cloth, and a wedding band more than gold. Here at the Lord's table we enter into relationship, "have communion" in the deepest sense. We fellowship with the risen Lord who is spiritually present in our hearts and in our worship. As we take the bread and cup in faith, we enter the divine Presence. We also have fellowship with other born-again believers who sit about the Lord's table with us. The observance is a vertical communion with God and a horizontal fellowship with our fellow Christians. In a third sense, we can say we have fellowship with the church triumphant, the saints in heaven. The epistle to the Hebrews reminds us of God's grandstand in glory. The redeemed of earlier ages are watching how we run. They are concerned about how we live and share the faith. Thus, we see that the Supper is a threefold fellowship: with the risen Christ, with our fellow believers, and with the redeemed in glory.

## III. The Lord's Supper Is Eschatological—It Points to the End Time

Eschatology has to do with the end of history and the return of Christ. It is the doctrine of last things. Interestingly, the Lord's Supper has this important future stance. We are told that we are to observe it "till he comes." Matthew quoted Jesus as saying, "For this is my blood of the covenant, which is poured out for many for the forgiveness of sins. I tell you I shall not drink again of this fruit of the vine until that day when I drink it new with you in my Father's kingdom" (Matt. 26:28-29). At the table we not only look back to the historical Christ-event we also look forward to Christ's return at the close of history. Then the church triumphant, the redeemed of all time will worship in the very presence of the Lord at the messianic banquet in heaven.

The Lord's Supper is historical; it recalls his cross. It is mystical; it celebrates his presence with us. And it is eschatological; it anticipates his triumphant return at the end of the age.

Come, let us celebrate all this, here at the Lord's table.

## 23. The Supper as Thanksgiving

"He took bread and gave thanks" (Luke 22:19, KJV).

One of the names for the Lord's Supper is the Eucharist. This is simply a transliteration of the Greek word for thanks or thanksgiving. It reflects the note of joy and celebration in our observance. As we approach the Lord's table we are thankful for many things.

We give thanks for the good earth, created by our heavenly Father. I once read an adaptation of Psalm 34:1. "I will bless the Lord at all times; his praise shall continually be in my mouth." It had been turned into verse and printed in a Christmas card which read:

> Throughout all the changing scenes of life
>     In trouble and in joy,
> The praises of my God shall still
>     My heart and tongue employ.

We are also thankful for God's generous provision of our every need. He provides "our daily bread," those things without which life would be hard or impossible. More than that, he provides the answer to our higher hunger. Jesus said, "Blessed are those who hunger and thirst after righteousness." And the psalmist sang, "He restores my soul." Still further, God gives us all of life's extras: color, sound, beauty, a baby's smile, love's embrace. Thank God for his adequate provision and providential care.

The Lord's Supper brings our thanksgiving into focus, "He took bread . . . and gave thanks." It reminds us of his great gift—his body and blood given for us. The only appropriate response to his grace is gratitude.

Consider Jesus' personal situation when he gave thanks in the upper room. His own family thought him mad and his brothers came to take him home to Nazareth. He had become an embarrassment to them. His disciples were bickering selfishly. His enemies were plotting his death at that very hour. How could he have been more misunderstood? Jesus was on the threshold of Gethsemane and within the shadow of Calvary. Didn't he have every right to feel depression and despair? And yet the Scripture tells us that he took the bread and cup and gave thanks to his heavenly Father. Little wonder then that the Supper focuses our thanksgiving.

We have every reason for giving thanks. Christ died to deliver us from the tyranny of sin. He is present with us here in our worship. And he is coming again at the end of time, to take us to be with him forever.

The hymn writer, Matthias Claudius, caught this glad note in his song "We Plow the Fields, and Scatter."

> We plow the fields and scatter
> The good seed on the land,
> But it is fed and watered
> By God's almighty hand.
> He sends the snow in the winter,
> The warmth to swell the grain,
> The breezes and the sunshine,
> And soft refreshing rain.
> We thank thee, then, O Father,
> For all things bright and good,
> The seedtime and the harvest
> Our life, our health, our food;
> Accept the gifts we offer
> For all Thy love imparts,
> And, what Thou most desirest,
> Our humble, thankful hearts.

*Refrain*
All good gifts around us
Are sent from heaven above;
Then thank the Lord,
O thank the Lord
For all His Love.

## 24. *Sacramentum*—Oath of Loyalty

Many Christian groups call the Lord's Supper by the name *sacrament*. Obviously, such a term is defined in different ways. Perhaps the most common understanding of the word is that the Supper is a sacrament in the sense that it is "a means of grace." Its observance is considered by some to be a saving act. It is believed that in taking communion the worshiper somehow appropriates God's grace almost magically. Most, if not all, Baptists would argue that this is not a biblical view of the Lord's Supper. We do not see the observance as a saving means of grace. We might be more prone to use "sacrament" if it were defined as a symbol of Christ's body and blood, and if we could use the term with its original meaning.

The word comes from the Latin term *sacramentum*. It was originally applied to a pledge, some security, or a bond posted in court. Later, it came to be used of the Roman soldier's oath of loyalty to his commanding officer or the emperor. It was his oath of allegiance to be repeated annually. Augustine interpreted the word applied to the Lord's Supper as a sign or symbol. Thus, we can call the Supper a symbol or a sacrament. The terms may be used synonomously.

A sacrament is some common object which has a meaning beyond itself. It could be a keepsake or an heirloom. The object may be worthless on the market but invaluable to an individual or group.

A symbol, or sacrament, can be an object like a wedding ring. Its monetary value may be small and yet have great value to the couple for it represents a sacred relationship. Or the American flag is only a few dollars worth of cloth, but it stands for the nation. By a similar token the elements of the Lord's Supper are simply bread and the fruit of the vine. But these common ingredients have a sacramental significance in that they symbolize or stand for the body and blood of Christ. The Supper is a symbolic meal and in that sense could be called a sacrament. This does not mean or imply that the Supper is some kind of means of grace for our salvation. Actually, Christ himself is the supreme sacrament, he is the Word of God in flesh.

## I. The Supper Is an Act of Loyalty

As we observe the ordinance we pledge our allegiance to Jesus Christ. We promise him our loyalty and affirm our fidelity. Coming to the table, we are confronted by the risen Christ and his ethical claims on us. We are reminded of the seriousness of our sin. It is an offense against love. The Supper calls on us to confess our sins and receive Christ's forgiveness. Our table worship results in praise and gratitude for divine grace; it is a time for adoration. Here, as a new Christian taking the Lord's Supper for the first time, we pledge our loyalty to Christ. In subsequent services we renew our vows to him. Just as we pledge our allegiance to the nation, using the symbol of the flag, so we affirm our loyalty to Christ in our observance at the table. It is a symbolic or sacramental worship experience.

## II. The Supper Results in a Life of Obedience

Here at the Lord's table we confront the will of God for our life. It is a time for our commitment to obey him.

The period of self-examination which precedes the Supper affords us an opportunity to let our will be conformed to his.

At the Lord's table we also commit ourselves to live a righteous life. This has both a negative thrust and a positive side. We determine to avoid evil and we promise to fill our life with that which is good, noble, and pure. Paul wrote, "Finally, brethren, whatsoever things are true, whatsoever things are honest, whatsoever things are just, whatsoever things are pure, whatsoever things are lovely, whatsoever things are of good report; if there be any virtue, and if there be any praise, think on these things" (Phil. 4:8, KJV).

Let us therefore observe the Lord's Supper as an oath of loyalty, a pledge of allegiance, an act of dedication.

Hear the invitation to the table:

> Come to this sacred Table, not because you must but because you may; come not to testify that you are righteous, but that you sincerely love our Lord Jesus Christ, and desire to be his true disciples: come, not because you are strong, but because you are weak; not because you have any claim on heaven's rewards, but because in your frailty and sin you stand in constant need of heaven's mercy and help." [5]

Christ has made some precious pledges to us. He said, "I will not leave you comfortless, I will come to you."

In silent prayer, will you pledge your love to him?

## 25. Man from Emmaus

A MONOLOGUE
Luke 24:13-49

The year is A.D. 55. The place is the meeting of the congregation of believers in Antioch, Syria. The pastor has invited Cleopas to give his testimony before the observance of the Lord's Supper:

"Thank you dear friend. How gracious of you to invite me to share in your worship. I bring you greetings from those of the Way in Emmaus. Say, I like your new name for believers here in Antioch—'Christians'—how appropriate, for indeed we do strive to be like Christ in attitude and love.

"I am happy to share my testimony with you. When I entered the courtyard and saw the table prepared for observance of the Supper, my mind went back instantly to that night in Emmaus when

Mary and I watched the Master bless and break bread in our home. Let me tell you about it.

"Emmaus is a village seven miles northwest of Jerusalem. Warm springs there have made it something of a resort. We local residents are convinced that the mineral waters are healthful and curative. On the afternoon of the first day of the week my wife, Mary, and I were walking from Jerusalem home. As we walked the setting sun appeared as a bronze disk above the Mediterranean horizon.

"Recent days had been pregnant with staggering events. We had been in the throng when Jesus entered Jerusalem in triumph. We were recounting sadly all that had happened to our leader during the past week of controversy, his arrest, trials, execution, and burial. Mary had been at the cross and I had seen his limp, pierced body as it was laid in the tomb of Joseph of Arimathea by Nicodemus.

"What puzzled us most was the strange report we had heard earlier that day: the women had visited the tomb that morning only to find it empty. They returned to our disciple group with tales of having seen angels. Two of our band, Peter and John, verified their story of the empty tomb, but none of them saw the Master. 'It takes more than an empty tomb to verify a resurrection,' I argued. Mary intuitively felt that the women must be correct. Still, both of us could not understand why God had allowed the cross and had not delivered Jesus. We were not alone on the road. We were joined by a third person, a stranger, as we walked along. How long he went unnoticed, I cannot say. We were so absorbed in our own grief and perplexity. I'm afraid much of what we felt was self-pity.

"Tactfully, he inquired, 'What is this you are arguing about?' I stopped still in my tracks. My amazement had to be apparent. I asked, 'Are you the only visitor, the only pilgrim, in Jerusalem who has not heard of the recent events there?'

" 'What events?' he asked. I recounted the arrest, trials, and execution by our chief priests and leaders of Jesus of Nazareth, a prophet who spoke with power. I said, 'We had hoped that he would be the one to deliver us and liberate Israel from the tyrant's heel. But now all our hopes are crushed, and it has been three days since his crucifixion. Some women who belong to our group found his tomb empty, but they must simply be hysterical.' Out of the corner of my eye, I saw Mary giving me a strange look. 'But,' said I convincingly, 'they did not see Jesus.' The most shattering disappointment is to be disappointed in the Christ.

"Then he said, 'You appear blind to the truth and slow to believe what the prophets wrote. Surely, the Messiah had to suffer before entering his glory.'

"The stranger sounded a bit audacious! Yet, there was a compelling ring of authority in what he said and the way in which he said it. One simply had to listen to him.

"He began with Moses and went through the prophets explaining the Scriptures which referred to the Messiah and his suffering. It was as if the fog was gradually lifting, and our understanding was coming clear for the first time. Strange, you know. We had actually heard much of this before, but now we were beginning to see how it all fitted together.

"All too soon it seemed, we reached Emmaus and our modest home. The stranger was courteous, saying he would go on further before stopping for the night. But we insisted that he stay with us, since it was nearly dark. 'Don't go, it is getting dark; you can see the first stars. Come in, stay with us,' said Mary. He consented and accepted our hospitality. (How glad I've always been that he did.)

"Mary busied herself in the kitchen preparing some food. We had been so upset that we had not eaten since early that morning. I sat in the other room with the stranger, asking further explanation of certain Scriptures he had quoted. The idea of a suffering Messiah was alien to all we'd ever been taught or heard preached at the synagogue. We had to unlearn in order to learn anew. It took a bit of getting used to.

"Presently Mary called us to the kitchen. On the table she had dinner spread: cold lamb, olives, bread, and figs. We asked him to take the place of honor and serve as host.

"You know God comes to us also in the midst of our ordinary everyday life, not only in worship and crisis. He came to Moses while he was at his work as a shepherd; to Mary while she was about her housework; to Peter mending his nets; and to Saul on a journey. Little did we realize that he was about to burst into our lives at the dinner table! He is Lord of the dinner table as well as of the communion table. He is as much the head of our homes as head of his body the church.

"He took the loaf of bread, said the blessing, and broke it in pieces, passing it to us.

"Suddenly, we saw! We recognized him! The grace he offered had a traditional tone, but his manner, his gestures, his hands—there were *scars* in his hands! The words were the same as when he fed the multitudes beside the sea! It was the Lord Jesus! It was true! He was risen from the dead, alive!

"Just as suddenly as we recognized him, he was gone! We looked at each other in startled disbelief. You know how it is with a husband and wife. You know each other so well that you know what the other is thinking and about to say. Simultaneously we exclaimed, 'Didn't our hearts feel strangely warm within us, as he explained the Scriptures to us on the road?'

"Then and there, we took some food in hand, put on our coats and began walking back to Jerusalem. This was news too good to keep! Our fatigue was forgotten in the joy and excitement of this new discovery!

"We had thought that he would liberate Israel. Now we realized that as the risen Christ he would redeem the world and everyone in it who will believe!

"We found the eleven and other disciples at John Mark's mother's house west of the Temple area. They were talking excitedly about the Lord's having appeared to Simon.

"We told our story almost simultaneously, one hardly waiting for the other to stop, to relate some fresh detail. We told them how we knew it was the Lord when he broke the bread at our table.

"While we were still talking, Jesus stood in our midst. We fell back in awe as he said, 'God's peace be with you.' We were startled! Some thought him a ghost or spirit of some kind.

" 'Don't be alarmed,' he said. 'Look at my hands and feet. See, it is really I. Feel the wounds and see for yourselves. A ghost does not have flesh and blood as I have.' Most were obviously unconvinced. He said, 'Have you anything here to eat?' Andrew gave him some cooked fish, and he ate it before us.

"He explained the Scriptures further, especially those passages about the Suffering Servant in Isaiah. He said the Messiah must suffer and rise from the dead on the third day, and that repentance which leads to the forgiveness of sins must be proclaimed to all the nations in his name. He told us to wait in Jerusalem until we were clothed with power from on high.

"I wish I could tell you of his ascension and the coming of the Holy Spirit on Pentecost, but time will not permit just now.

"Ah, it is true, my fellow Christians. Christ is risen, alive, 'let loose in the world' as the centurion said to Pilate's wife. This gives us reasons for comfort, joy and hope! His Presence may be realized any time, any place—surely at the Lord's Supper. Remember his promise, 'Lo, I am with you alway' (Matt. 28:20). It's always possible for believers to meet him. Come, let us break bread together.

"It is not my voice I would have you hear now, but that of the risen Christ. Jesus said at his ascension, 'All power is given unto me in heaven and in earth' (Matt. 28:18). He also said, 'I am come that they might have life, and that they might have it more abundantly' (John 10:10). Again he said, 'If any man . . . open the door, I will come in' (Rev. 3:20).

"We belive his promises and accept his invitation. Even so, come, Lord Jesus. Amen."

## 26. The Word Made Visible
### (A CHRISTMAS EVE MEMORIAL MEDITATION)

For to us a child is born, to us a son is given; and the government will be upon his shoulder, and his name will be called "Wonderful Counselor, Mighty God, Everlasting Father, Prince of Peace" (Isa. 9:6).

For to you is born this day in the city of David a Savior, who is Christ the Lord (Luke 2:11).

Now as they were eating, Jesus took bread, and blessed, and broke it, and gave it to the disciples and said, "Take, eat; this is my body." And he took a cup, and when he had given thanks he gave it to them, saying, "Drink of it, all of you" (Matt. 26:26-27).

John's Gospel tells us that the Word of God was made visible in the person of Jesus Christ. This logos or cosmic Christ was co-creator of the world, along with God the Father and the Holy Spirit. Yet, he entered history and became a tiny baby, nursing at Mary's breast. He was a child prodigy at twelve, stumping the doctors of the Law at the Temple in Jerusalem. He was the matchless Teacher whose words and ideas are deeply inbedded in our Western culture. He became the Suffering Servant, bleeding and broken on a felon's cross. He was raised from the dead by the power of God. This Word who was made visible is real and alive today.

This Word who was made visible in the manger and on the cross is here in our midst on this Christmas Eve. His presence is represented in the bread and cup on the table. Theologian Emil Brunner considered the Lord's Supper to be an illustrated or visible word of God. These simple elements are signs and reminders that he is with us still. Here at the table the good news of Bethlehem and the empty tomb is demonstrated and celebrated. We say, "I'd rather see a sermon than hear one any day." Then look!

Christmas means that God has intervened on our behalf. Christ has come into the world to make peace, to save us from our sins, and to reconcile us to God. We who believe on this living Word have been saved from the penalty of our sins. We are being saved day by day from the power of sin in our lives. One day we will be saved from the very presence of evil and temptation.

Christ is born—rejoice!

Christ is here—give thanks!

Christ is coming again—lift up your heads, your redemption draws near.

Many Christians have stood in the grotto or cave in Bethlehem where they claim Jesus was born. It is a pilgrim experience to feel his presence there and realize anew how historical our faith really is. However, we can be just as keenly aware that our Lord is with us here—in our worship at his table miles away and centuries after his birth. He told the disciples that it was to their advantage for him to go away that the Holy Spirit might come. That sounded ironic, but we know that is true for we have met the Christ, not in some distant land, but right here where we live. The poet wrote:

> Shakespeare is dust, and will not come
> To question from his Avon tomb,
> And Socrates and Shelley keep
> An Attic and Italian sleep
> ................................................................
> They see not. But, O Christians, who
> Throng Holborn and Fifth Avenue,
> May you not meet, in spite of death,
> A traveler from Nazareth? [6]

Christ has come. Christ is here. Let us worship him and rejoice.

## 27. The Upper Room in Three Acts
John 13:1; 20:19-20, 24; Acts 1:13; 2:1-4

Charles Templeton once said that the history of the world was altered by the events which took place in two upper rooms. They were separated by some three thousand miles and nearly two thousand years.

One was a flat over a laundry in the Soho slum district of London. It had a dirty, curtainless window, and it contained a small, round table stacked high with papers. By the light of a flickering oil lamp a bearded man sat writing with a cheap, scratchy pen. He was Karl Marx, a Jew, and he was writing *Das Kapital* the bible of modern Communism. Today nearly half the world's population follows his economic theory, and most live in slavery as bad as that against which they rebelled.

The second upper room was spacious and was located in one of the world's oldest cities, Jerusalem. There a large table was set for thirteen men to eat the Passover feast together. On the table were lamb, bread, wine, and herbs. After the meal was concluded, their leader Jesus instituted a symbolic Supper which has been observed by millions all over the world, for nearly two hundred centuries. We believe it will continue to be the focal point of Christian worship, in observances simple and elaborate, till the end of time.

Other events of momentous significance also took place in that upper room in Jerusalem. Think back.

## Act I—Jesus' Last Supper

All readers of the Gospels are familiar with the events of the last week of Jesus' life, and the events of that evening. Momentous debates had crowded in on Jesus since his triumphal entry to the Holy City on the previous Sunday. Excitement had run high in his disciple band. Now he had eaten the Passover with them for the last time. After Judas went out, Jesus had instituted the Memorial Supper by which he would always be remembered. A long, teaching discourse took up most of the evening. Jesus spoke words of comfort to prepare the disciples for what would follow after his departure (John 14). He taught them utter dependence on him in the parable of the true vine (John 15). He promised to send them the Holy Spirit (John 16) and he prayed the great high priestly prayer for his disciples and for us (John 17). What a scene; what a night to remember; what a sacred spot!

## Act II—Tragedy Turns to Triumph

Following Jesus' arrest, trials, and crucifixion, the disciples gathered again in the upper room. They had heavy hearts. The past three days had been unbelievably tragic. Their hope had died with the Master. The dream of the kingdom now appeared impossible. Ten disciples huddled there in fear. The door was barred. Thomas was absent and Judas had committed suicide by hanging. The men spoke in hushed tones. They were Jesus' followers and closest friends. He had been executed by the authorities, and they might very well be next!

Suddenly they were aware of another in the midst, and they became more frightened than before. Then this figure spoke in a familiar voice, "Peace be unto you." He showed them his pierced hands and side and they knew it was Jesus. "Then were the disciples glad, when they saw the Lord." It was true, those strange stories about the women having seen him at the garden tomb. He was risen, alive, really returned from the dead. And this remarkable appearance took place in the same upper room where they had eaten with the Master.

## Act III—The Day the Power Came

The risen Christ continued to appear to those who loved him: again on the next Sunday in the upper room, this time with Thomas present. He appeared to the disciples and to several hundred people in Galilee. Then after forty days he ascended to heaven.

Jesus promised that if he went away the Holy Spirit would come. Thus, the early church met for prayer in the same upper room (Acts 1:14). On the feast of Pentecost they were gathered when the sound of heaven entered the place and they were all filled with the Holy Spirit. Inspired, they went out and bore witness to their faith and the inbreaking of the kingdom of God.

Three great chapters in Christian history were written in that upper room of John Mark's mother's house: the Lord's Supper was instituted by Jesus; the risen Christ appeared to his disciples; and the Holy Spirit came upon the embryonic church with power. It is remarkable. Yet, we worship not a place but a person. As surely as he was present in that upper room both before and after his death, so he is here with us in this place of worship. And the same Holy Spirit is here to save and empower us. Jesus has given us this magnificent legacy. We appropriate it by faith.

Listen now as the organ and piano play "Jesu, Joy of Man's Desiring."

## 28. Profession and Practice
### (A NEW YEAR'S COMMUNION MEDITATION)

Now, what do you think? There was a man who had two sons. He went to the older one and said, "Son, go work in the vineyard today." "I don't want to," he answered, but later he changed his mind and went to the vineyard. Then the father went to the other son and said the same thing. "Yes, sir," he answered, but he did not go. Which one of the two did what his father wanted? "The older one," they answered. "And I tell you this," Jesus said to them. "The tax collectors and the prostitutes are going into the Kingdom of God ahead of you. For John The Baptist came to you showing you the right path to take, and you would not believe him, but the tax collectors and the prostitutes believed him. Even when you saw this you did not change your minds later on and believe him" (Matt. 21:28-32, TEV).

This is the season of the year when we make promises, vows, resolutions. We determine that we will watch our diet, cutting down on sweets, starches, and fats (lest we become fat). We may resolve to get more exercise, stop smoking, or begin studying in the second semester. We promise that we will have a better attitude toward the boss, the coach, and our mother-in-law. It seems appropriate then to consider this parable of Jesus which has to do with promises kept and not kept, at the beginning of the new year.

The setting is this: Jesus had entered the city of Jerusalem in triumph on Palm Sunday—to the accolades of the crowd, the delight of his disciples, and the despair of his enemies. Then the Master proceeded to cleanse the Temple of its coin exchangers and merchants selling sacrificial birds and animals. The religious establishment was enraged! After all, the high priest himself had authorized the stalls in the Temple courtyard (and he received a commission from their transactions). They demanded to know "by what authority" Jesus had done this.

Jesus answered his enemies by asking them a question. By what authority had John the Baptist preached—man's or God's? This question put his enemies in a dilemma. If they said by man's authority, the populace would have come up in arms. If they replied that John was sent from God, Jesus would have asked, why then had they not believed John's message? When his enemies could give no answer, Jesus told this parable. Its meaning is crystal clear and the story is true to life.

## I. The Parable

The "man" in Jesus' story is obviously God. Jesus spoke of God so simply. Theologians and philosophers seem to delight in speaking of him obscurely, as the First Cause and the Ground of all being. Preachers also like to address him in high-flown titles such as the Eternal. Jesus spoke of God in vivid word pictures. He taught us that God is like a gifted Gardener, a faithful Shepherd, and a loving Father.

The "two sons" were asked to work in the father's vineyard. The boys' responses were totally different. The religious type replied politely, "I go, Sir"—but didn't. He represents the pillars of the church whose profession sounds impressive, but whose practice falls short of what is asked. The older son represents the religious outcasts, the publicans (Jewish collectors of Roman taxes, a despised lot) and the harlots (who were the social and religious scum). This boy said, "No, I won't go," but later repented and went to work in the vineyard.

Jesus asked which son did his father's will. Obviously, it was the first. Then Jesus said that publicans and prostitutes were entering the kingdom ahead of these religious folk!

## II. Both Sons Were Wrong

Jesus did not actually commend either. The second boy was wrong to promise but not go. The first was wrong to refuse, though he later went.

We all loathe a hypocrite, one who pretends to be something he is not; one who promises but does not practice. Perhaps the classic example of a hypocrite in literature is Robert Burns' "Holy Willie."

In one of his poems, Burns gives us "Holy Willie's Prayer":

> O Thou that in the heavens does dwell
> What, as it pleases best Thyself,
> Sends one to Heaven and ten to hell
>     All for Thy glory,
> And not for one good or ill
>     They've done before Thee!
>
> I bless and praise Thy matchless might
> When thousands Thou hast left in night,
> That I am here before thy sight
>     for gifts and grace
> A burning and a shining light
>     To all this place.
>
> Yet I am here a chosen sample,
> To show Thy grace is great and ample
> I'm here a pillar of Thy temple,
>     Strong as a rock,
> A guide, a buckler and example
>     To all Thy folk.[7]

Willie actually lived in Scotland in Burns' time. His name was William Fisher. He was a farmer who spied on sabbath-breakers and reported them to the judge. Yet Willie himself stole church offerings, ruined several country girls, and died in a ditch during a snowstorm while in a drunken stupor. A hypocrite certainly does harm to the reputation of the church and the cause of Christ.

However, let me remind you that there are hypocrites outside the church as well. Some people delight to appear hard-boiled, irreligious men of the world—when all the while they have a big heart and live by a better ethic than they profess. Many of them have a secret respect for true religion but lack the courage to profess faith; so they pretend to be worse than they are. (Isn't that hypocritical, too?) They ought to come out for Christ, repent, and give themselves to do the will of God.

## III. Application of the Parable

Talk alone is cheap. Promises without performance, fine words without deeds to back them up, will not cut it. There is no substitute for the obedient life.

We sometimes think about what it would be like to meet Jesus in the flesh. To be sure, it would be wonderful. But it would also be frightening. Suppose he asked if we are living obediently, if we are taking him and his teachings seriously, if we are living by the ethic of *agape* love. He has asked us not simply to believe in him. He has also asked that we work for him. Our deeds demonstrate our love. Recall how the knights asked for the hardest tasks by which to prove their devotion.

This parable contains both a warning and a promise. We are warned that despite our professions of faith and love, if we fail to perform we can become castaways. There is also the bright promise: if we repent and do the Father's will, we are accepted. Jesus said, "Not every one who says to me, 'Lord, Lord,' shall enter the kingdom of heaven, but he who does the will of my Father who is in heaven" (Matt. 7:21).

Love is something we do. Let us make our vows here at the Lord's table. Then let us keep our promises in the New Year.

*Benediction:* "Go in joy;
          Sin no more
          Love God.
          Serve His children.
              Amen."

## 29. He Is Alive!
(EASTER COMMUNION)
John 20:1-20, NEB

This morning as dawn makes its way over the rim of the earth, millions waken to celebrate the grandest event of human history. Today is V-Day, Victory Day—He is alive! The resurrection of Jesus Christ, not the landing on the moon, is the greatest victory in history.

One summer I visited Napoleon's tomb in Paris. At its base in the royal chapel the names of all the general's victories are inscribed (one searches in vain for the battle of Waterloo). All the victories of Alexander, Caesar, Napoleon, and Hitler fade in the memory, while Christ's resurrection is celebrated every Lord's Day.

It is celebrated this Easter morning from New York's Fifth Avenue to thatched-roofed African huts; from frozen Greenland to the South Sea Islands; from the baroque Gothic cathedrals of Europe to the plain Quaker meeting houses of the Midwest. We gather in five hundred thousand churches on every continent. We praise the risen Christ in two thousand languages in gatherings of Christians numbering from three to three thousand. All declare, "He is alive! Now is Christ risen! Risen, indeed!"

This warring world is living on the wrong side of Easter. The radical theologians proclaimed the death of God prematurely. Our protest has grown from a whisper to a shout!

## I. The Resurrection Is a Fact of History

In 1962, Leonard Small of Edinburgh delivered a series of Holy Week messages on the BBC entitled, "Lift Up Your Heart!" He received an abusive letter: "I challenge you to prove that Jesus Christ ever lived, much less rose again from the dead. Dead men do not rise. You have no right, in such a world as this, to bid us 'Lift Up Our Hearts.'"

A knowledgeable historian will tell you that we have more historical evidence for the life of Christ than for that of Julius Caesar!

Many arguments have been advanced against the historicity of the resurrection. Some point out that there are discrepancies in the Gospel accounts. But if the four writers had given identical accounts that would prove collusion! You never signed your name the same twice in your life. Two identical signatures mean that one must be forged! Differences in the Gospel writers' accounts do not disprove the resurrection.

Others accept the ancient lie that Jesus' body was stolen from the grave. This argument has difficulties. If it had been stolen by Jesus' enemies, they could have later produced it and stopped Christianity cold. Did the disciples steal the body and preach the resurrection as a known hoax? If that were so, they would not have died for a known lie. Nobody produced the dead body of Jesus, because there was no body to produce. He was risen, and his body was transformed.

Hugh J. Schonfield claims there was a Passover plot. According to this theory, Jesus swooned or passed out on the cross. He was taken down for dead and was buried. In the cool tomb Jesus revived. He then went to his disciples and announced that he has been raised. There are serious difficulties with the swoon theory. If he revived inside the tomb, how did he move the massive stone over the entrance to the cave? How did he get out of the winding sheet in which he was buried? Think what an anticlimax Jesus' eventual death would have created for his disciples!

Still others have suggested that "tear-blinded" Mary really did see the gardener near the tomb and mistook him for Jesus. But how do you explain the risen Christ's appearance to the two at Emmaus, to the ten apostles, to Thomas, to Peter in Galilee, to James, and to five hundred believers who saw him? He was real and alive. He was no phantom. He ate with them; they heard his familiar voice. He is alive!

The ironic thing is that the disciples did not expect the resurrection—or they would have been waiting outside the tomb. They would not have come to embalm his body. They would not have returned to their fishing. They would not have despaired saying, "We had hoped that he was the one to redeem Israel" (Luke 24:21). Once the resurrection was reported to the disciples they did not believe it. They had to be convinced by the appearances of the risen Christ.

The existence of the church, changed and convinced men, is proof of the resurrection. Elton Trueblood writes, "The primary evidence provided by the apostles is not what they said, but what they became." The cowardly disciples became courageous. These men whose hopes had been dashed like Dresden on granite were transformed. They sang and preached the gospel, and they died triumphantly in the faith. The resurrection is a fact of history.

## II. The Resurrection Is an Experience of Life

The risen Christ is alive, here, now! None of the apostles "remembered" Jesus. They had no need to. In John Masefield's drama the Roman centurion reports Jesus' crucifixion and the disappearance of his body to Pilate. Procula, the governor's wife, asks the soldier, "Do you think he is dead?" "No, lady, I don't," he replies. "Then where is he?" she asks. "Let loose in the world, lady," is the centurion's opinion. It's true! The Holy Spirit is carrying out Jesus' ongoing ministry in the world today. Acts 1:1 tells us about "all that Jesus *began* to do and to teach." [8]

Albert Schweitzer wrote: "He comes to us, as of old he came to them by the lakeside, and he says to us, 'Follow me.' " The resurrection is an experience of life.

## III. The Resurrection Is Our Hope of Glory

"Because I live, you shall live also," said Jesus Christ. By his resurrection he defeated death, the last enemy. His resurrection was not the mere resuscitation of a corpse, which would die again. His was no limited victory but a complete one. His physical body was transformed into an unlimited spiritual one. He was thus fitted for another dimension. Yet his new body was a real one—they touched him and he ate in their presence.

Christ lived and died and was raised to life by the power of God. Therefore, raised to life by the power of God, by faith in him, we, too, can conquer death.

Helmut Thielicke sounded like Hamlet when he wrote, "When I die, if someone finds my skull, may that skull preach to him:

'I have no eyes, yet I see Him;
I have no brain, yet I know Him;
I have no tongue, yet I praise Him;
I lie without in the church yard,
Yet I am within Paradise!' " [9]

Is that poetic fantasy? I think not, for Jesus said, He that believeth in me, though he were dead, yet shall he live. Whosoever liveth and believeth in me shall never die. (John 11:25-26, KJV).

Hallelujah! He is alive! It's true!

Do you believe in him? If not, trust him—now.
Let us come to the Lord's table, worship, and celebrate!

# 30. The Supper and the Shepherd Psalm
## PSALM 23

There is a vast ignorance of the Bible, even among church folk.
One fellow thought Dan and Beersheba were brother and sister.
Our entering college students do not know their Bible. Sixty percent
cannot name the four Gospels—Matthew, Mark, Luke, and John.
Ninety-six percent of them cannot write the Ten Commandments.
The professor thought one girl had written them correctly. A careful
reading, however, had the Seventh Commandment: "Thou shalt not
*admit* adultery."

Psalm 23 is simple, yet profound. Almost everyone knows it from
memory, yet there are spiritual riches there still untapped.

With a little imagination we can see David as he wrote this psalm.
It was a cool night with a star-filled Judean sky. You could see
five thousand stars in the clear sky. Some appeared so close that
you felt you could rake them down by stretching your arms. The
day with its grazing and search for water was over. The sheep were
huddled in sleep. But the shepherd kept a watchful eye for predatory
wild animals.

The campfire embers were fanned by the night breeze and glowed
red again. Listen. Did you hear it? It was the ancient sound of a
shepherd's flute, followed by a melodic Hebrew song. David's heart
fairly burst with the joy of God's presence. His feelings overflowed
in a psalm.

Who would have thought that psalm of simple trust would be
the subject of worship in a church service—three thousand years
later? David's psalm is a personal affirmation of faith. In our Bible

it is preceded by Psalm 22: a song of deep anguish, whose words came to Jesus' lips in his last hour on the cross. "My God, my God, why hast thou forsaken me?" (Matt. 27:46).

Psalm 24, by contrast, is a song of triumph: "The earth is the LORD's and the fullness thereof; The world and they that dwell therein. Lift up your heads, O ye gates. And the King of glory shall come in" (vv. 1, 7, KJV).

Psalm 23 is the bridge over troubled waters, which leads from anguish to triumph. The psalm is realistic. It is no sundial recording sunny hours only. It reminds us of dark hours as well, from which we are not immune. The twenty-third Psalm promises God's presence in both good and bad times.

Note that the psalm shows us—

## I. God Is Our Shepherd (vv. 1-4)

"The Lord is my shepherd" is a reminder that God provides for our needs. We are his flock—the company of the God-led.

Many ancient people thought of their king as the shepherd of the nation. As an example, Pharaoh Tutankhamen's inner sarcophagus is a golden representation of the king with his hands across his chest. One hand holds a flail or whip, symbol of authority. The other hand holds a shepherd's crook, symbol of his benevolent role as the shepherd of Egypt.

David called the Lord his shepherd. Second, Isaiah saw God in the same way for he wrote: "He shall feed his flock like a shepherd: he shall gather the lambs with his arm, and carry them in his bosom, and shall gently lead those who are with young" (40:11, KJV).

To call God "my Shepherd" means "I shall not want." God provides "green pastures" (no easy task in Palestine) and "still waters" (the shepherd would place a small dam across a wadi to catch rainwater and form a pool). Jesus taught us to pray for "our daily bread." God not only provides our material needs, but he "restores my soul" as well. He answers the believer's deepest spiritual need with gentle delights and the joy of salvation. He satisfies our higher hunger—to know God.

David also sang of Yahweh, "He leadeth me." We do believe

in providence and divine guidance. Otherwise our life would be little more than "a tale told by an idiot, full of sound and fury, signifying nothing."

To say the Lord is my Shepherd also means I shall not fear, "though I walk through the valley of the shadow of death." The Scots call it the "gloomy glen" and the Hebrew can be translated "deep darkness." How can a man face the king of terrors without ultimate fear? In the knowledge that "Thou art with me." The shepherd's rod and staff were a comfort to the sheep. They were weapons—stern stuff—but they were for the sheep's protection.

I don't want you to misunderstand. This psalm is no sleepy pastoral scene. It does not describe mental or spiritual stagnation. This is not a psalm to rock us to sleep. Indeed, if you are looking for an easy way, you might as well not look in the Bible.

Psalm 23 is a call to pilgrimage—"I walk." It describes life with God en route. We are to listen for God's voice, and follow his leading.

The psalm also declares—

## II. The Lord Is Our Host (vv. 5-6)

The Lord is my host, and I am his guest. In verses 1-4, the psalmist said, "I walk" with my shepherd. In verses 5-6 he says, "I dwell" in his presence.

At breakfast one morning I told Dr. Elton Trueblood I planned to preach on Psalm 23. He said, "Be sure to note the change of person in the psalm." The psalmist begins by referring to God in the third person—"*He* leadeth me." Then he shifts to the second person. You cannot use the second person of someone unless he is present.

The metaphor shifts from shepherd and sheep to host and guest. Note the gracious hospitality of God as host. There is nothing quite like Near Eastern hospitality. I must confess that the graciousness of an Arab home exceeds Southern hospitality.

In the presence of God the psalmist was safe even from his enemies. Our enemies are temptations to cheat and be lazy and unkind.

God is generous—"my cup is overflowing abundance" or as the *Jerusalem Bible* translates the verse: "my cup brims over." God can be extravagant in his blessings to us—consider your good health, family, friends, plenty, and the beauty all about you.

There is no other place as blessed as God's presence. The Hebrew literally translated reads, "Goodness and mercy will pursue me." God is no reluctant deity. He is anxious to bless his children. A Scottish preacher preaching on this psalm said, "The Lord is my Shepherd, aye, and more than that, he has two fine collie dogs: Goodness and Mercy, and they will see us home at last." Mercy is *chesed*, God's unfailing covenant love toward us.

The psalm reaches its climax with the phrase, "I will dwell in the house of the Lord, for ever." This passage was used for centuries in Jewish worship. I feel sure they interpreted this literally, as the Temple. However, it has also been interpreted by Christians as a reference to heaven. To be where God is, will be enough.

Jesus knew and loved the twenty-third Psalm. Indeed, he applied it to himself. In John 10 we read, "I am the good shepherd: the good shepherd giveth his life for the sheep" (v. 11). Jesus is both the shepherd and the Lamb of God, our sacrifice. That is radical. David would never have thought of that—yet it's true.

Tell me, who is your shepherd? Is it the Lord?

Here at the Lord's table we celebrate his protection and care. As we prepare to continue our worship, listen to the hymn: "The King of Love, My Shepherd Is."

## Notes

1. Adapted and arranged by John Jacob Niles, published by G. Shirmer, Inc.

2. An Adaptation from William Barclay, *Prayers for the Christian Year* (London: SCM Press, 1964), p. 36.

3. William Barclay, *The Lord's Supper*, "The Invitation" (London: SCM Press, 1967), p. 119.

4. John Masefield, *The Everlasting Mercy* (London: Sidgwick & Jackson Ltd., 1911), p. 77.

5. Payne, Winward & Cox, *Minister's Worship Manual*, pp. 14-15.

6. John Drinkwater, *Masterpieces of Religious Verse*, ed. James Dalton Morrison, "To and Fro About the City" (New York: Harper & Row, 1948), p. 260.

7. Robert Burns, *Poetical Works of Robert Burns*, "Holy Willie" (London: W. & R. Chambers, 1958), p. 63.

8. Masefield, *op. cit.*

9. Helmut Thielicke, *The Silence of God* (Grand Rapids: Eerdmans', 1962), pp. 87-88.

# Selected Bibliography

BAILLIE, D. M. *The Theology of the Sacraments*. New York: Charles Scribner's Sons, 1957.

BARCLAY, WILLIAM. *The Lord's Supper*. London: SCM Press, 1967.

CAIRNS, DAVID. *In Remembrance of Me*. London: Goeffrey Bless, 1967.

CHRISTENSEN, JAMES L. *Creative Ways To Worship*. Old Tappan, N.J.: Fleming H. Revell, 1974.

——————. *New Ways to Worship*. Old Tappan, N.J.: Fleming H. Revell, 1973.

CLARK, JOHN G. *Meditations on the Lord's Supper*. Nashville: Broadman Press, 1958.

FOOTE, GASTON, Ed. *Communion Meditations*. Nashville: Abingdon Press, 1956.

FORD, D. W. CLEVERLY. *Preaching at the Parish Communion*. London: A. R. Mowbray & Co., 1967.

——————. *Preaching at the Parish Communion, 2*. London: A. R. Mowbray & Co., 1968.

GREET, BRIAN A. *Broken Bread in a Broken World*. Valley Forge: Judson Press, 1972.

GWYNNE, J. HAROLD. *Communion Meditations and Prayers*. Grand Rapids: Zondervan Publishing House, 1969.

HOON, PAUL WHITMAN. *The Integrity of Worship*. Nashville: Abingdon Press, 1971.

HUNTER, ARCHIBALD M. *Introducing New Testament Theology*. Philadelphia: Westminster Press, 1957.

JEREMIAS, JOACHIM. *The Eucharistic Words of Jesus*. London: SCM Press, 1966.

LUMPKIN, WILLIAM L. *Meditations for Communion Services*. Nashville: Abingdon Press, 1968.

MICKLEM, NATHANIEL, Ed. *Christian Worship*. Oxford University Press, 1936.

OGILVIE, LLOYD JOHN. *The Cup of Wonder*. Wheaton: Tyndale, 1976.

PEARCE, J. WINSTON. *Planning Your Preaching*. Nashville: Broadman Press, 1967.

PHILLIPS, J. B. *Appointment with God*. London: Epworth Press, 1954.

RANDOLPH, DAVID JAMES. *God's Party*. Nashville: Abingdon Press, 1975.

RICHARDSON, ALAN. *Introduction to the Theology of the New Testament*. New York: Harper & Brothers, 1958.

ROCHELLE, JAY C. *The Revolutionary Year*. Philadelphia: Fortress Press, 1973.

TURNBULL, RALPH G. *At the Lord's Table*. Grand Rapids: Baker Book House, 1967.

**Pastor's Manuals:**

BUTTRICK, DAVID. *The Worshipbook*. Philadelphia: Westminster Press, 1970.

DAVIES, HORTON AND SLIFER, MORRIS. *Prayers and Other Resources for Public Worship*. Nashville: Abingdon, 1976.

HOBBS, J. R. *The Pastor's Manual*. Nashville: Broadman Press, 1934.

PAYNE, WINWARD AND COX. *Minister's Worship Manual*. New York: World Publishing Co., 1969.

SEGLER, FRANKLIN M. *The Broadman Minister's Manual*. Nashville: Broadman Press, 1969.

**Journals and Monographs:**

DAVIES, G. HENTON. *Preaching the Lord's Supper*. London: 1967.

HOWARD, FRED D. *Interpreting the Lord's Supper*. Nashville: Broadman Press, 1966. O.P.

MCCALL, DUKE K., Ed. *What Is the Church?* Chapter 5: "The New Testament Significance of the Lord's Supper" by Dale Moody. Nashville: Broadman Press, 1958. O.P.

*Review and Expositor*. Vol. LXVI, No. 1. Winter, 1969.

The Sunday School *Illustrator*. Treatment of the Jewish Passover. Spring, 1976.

**Tapes:**

HENDRICKS, WILLIAM. "The Ordinances: A Baptist Perspective." *Update,* Vol. 3, No. 2, 1974.

MCLEOD, PETER. "Worshiping Through the Lord's Supper." Broadman Tape #447-165.